I0149294

Identifying Your Gifts and Service

(Small Group Edition)

Henry E. Neufeld

Energion Publications

http://www.energionpubs.com

Identifying Your Gifts and Service

(Small Group Edition)

Henry E. Neufeld

Cover Layout by Baxter's Elite Productions

www.baxterselite.com

This book incorporates portions of the following Participatory Study Series pamphlets, also written by Henry Neufeld: *I Want the Baptism of the Holy Spirit, Gifts and Offices*, and the entire *Spiritual Gifts* series, available free of charge at catalog.participatorystudyseries.com.

Energion Publications

P. O. Box 841

Gonzalez, FL 32560

Phone: (850) 968-1001

pubs@energion.com

http://www.energionpubs.com

Small Group Edition

ISBN: 1-893729-47-8

Table of Contents

PREFACE

The process for identifying one's gifts and place of service arises both from my experience teaching about the gifts of the Spirit and from my conviction that the key to identifying our gifts is in listening to the Holy Spirit.

Our Spiritual Gifts are characterized by being under the control of the one Spirit. This means that they come from one source, through the infilling of the Holy Spirit. It means, in addition, that the same Spirit has a place where we should use those gifts, and that the place in which we use them will be determined by how well it carries out the activities and goals that God has set for His church.

I strongly recommend a study of Paul's first letter to the Corinthian church along with looking at the ministry of Jesus in the gospels to show just how we are to minister. I discuss these issues more in my series of studies on 1 Corinthians, currently being presented online at the Pacesetters Bible School news blog (biblepacesetter.org/news, category *1 Corinthians*), and also in my series on the gifts of the Spirit presented at Springfield United Methodist Church in February of 2004, with audio also available on the same blog, category *Spiritual Gifts*.

Keeping our focus on Jesus and His ministry will open the doors to truly Spirit-filled and Spirit-directed ministry that builds the kingdom of God.

This new edition for small groups extends the concept of training the whole church so that a congregation can continue to involve new members in the process of discovery, so that every member will constantly be utilized to their fullest potential.

Henry Neufeld

Pensacola, FL

February, 2007

Dedication

To Perry and Anne Dalton, who first helped me understand the function of Spiritual Gifts in the church, and to the congregation of Springfield United Methodist Church, Florida, who allowed me to practice on them with much of this material.

ACKNOWLEDGMENTS

Besides those to whom I have dedicated this book, I want to thank my wife, Jody Neufeld, who has tirelessly written, proofread, edited and refined material on Spiritual Gifts both for this book and for numerous classes we have taught together. I am especially grateful to God for the power to go through with writing this book during a particularly difficult time of my life. He is faithful!

All errors that remain are, of course, mine.

Henry Neufeld

Gonzalez, Florida, February 7, 2007

Introduction

My earlier book, Identifying Your Gifts and Service (ISBN: 1-893729-27-3) is a handout designed for use with a church-wide program of discovering gifts and finding a place of service for every member. I designed it so that a teacher could present the various elements of the class, and the students could use the book as a collection of handouts. When I taught about spiritual gifts before I prepared that workbook I always had a stack of handouts that were clumsy and easy to lose, though not so easy to *use*.

I still recommend that if a church wants to identify and use the spiritual gifts of all their members, they should follow a program such as the one I designed and do so with as broad a group of members as possible. At the end of the program, the pastor and the church body have the opportunity to connect each person with an appropriate ministry in the church.

But what happens after that initial start? What about members who were unable to attend the program? What about new members who join the church?

That is the purpose of *Identifying Your Gifts and Service: Small Group Edition.* A small group, or even an individual working in cooperation with the church leadership can study this program and identify gifts and calling. I emphasize working with church leadership because this program is about listening to the Holy Spirit collectively, in the body. You can't do this book alone. It's about God's gifts to the whole church body.

In this book I will present all of the content of the first edition, along with chapters covering all of the lecture material. There are exercises and reading suggestions specifically for small group leaders who are preparing to lead this study and for the small group members. Portions of the program require the cooperation of church leadership. The ultimate goal is for every member to identify their gifts, and to connect with the local church body to find a place of service where they can put those gifts into action to build God's kingdom.

How to Use this Book

Purpose

This book is designed for use by a small group whose members want to discover their spiritual gifts and their place of service in the church body. I believe that the gifts are given by God and identified to us by God. This package is more about learning to listen to God and one another than it is about identifying which of a limited list of gifts and offices may be relevant to your call.

You will need to undertake this task in cooperation with your church's leadership. Your goal should be to enter active service using the gifts you discover during the program. If you do not use your gifts, not only will your ability to minister atrophy, your spiritual life will suffer as you hoard God's gracious gifts.

Calling

God's gifts always come with a call.

The scriptural foundation for this material is found in the resources list. This booklet provides the exercises and places to record the results of the various discussions. I do not intend the one survey provided as a means to identify what God has called you to do or how God has gifted you. When you have finished discussing what you have heard from the Lord, the survey is intended to help you focus on specifics and to help you see things that you might have missed because of preconceptions about your gifts and ministry.

If possible, get the leaders of your church to do a study with as many members of the congregation. Use this small group study to follow that up and to supplement. Teachers in the church can also use this book as a leader's guide, and then use the workbook (1-893729-27-3) as handouts for each church member.

The small group edition can also be used by a number of small groups simultaneously in order to get the whole church involved.

It is unlikely in most churches that you can get 100% participation, but that should always be your goal.

Organizing

Resources: A copy of this book for each group member, a Bible, and a pencil

People: Group leader, pastoral representative (pastor, associate, or assigned leader with the authority to speak for church leadership), 6-10 individuals who are ready to identify their gifts. The pastoral staff representative need not attend every session, but should be directly involved.

Time: Two hours (1 ½ to 2 hours per session). Don't rush, but keep detours to a minimum. Focus.

Prerequisites: An understanding of the gifts of the Spirit. Use some of the resources listed below in church teaching **prior to** the use of this program.

Lessons

As you look over the lessons you will notice that there are two chapters that are almost totally reading and content. These introduce the group to the basic concepts of spiritual gifts and prepares them for the exercises to follow. The remaining sessions are much more participatory in nature. Encourage the members of your group to read the material and prepare to be as actively involved as possible.

I suggest seven sessions, each of an hour and a half, as follows:

Chapter Title	Note
Introduction	Get your group organized, agree on leaders, especially if you plan to have different members lead different sessions.
The Holy Spirit and Spiritual Gifts	Learning session. It is best for every group member to read the chapter and supporting scriptures for themselves before beginning this session.
Spirit Led Ministry	Learning session. See above.
Identifying Your Gifts	Exercise session. There is some reading material, but the critical part of this session is working in

Chapter Title	Note
	small groups. Follow the instructions closely.
The Gifts Survey	Exercise session. Leave plenty of time to discuss results and do not be upset if group members criticize the survey. Dissatisfaction with the survey results can be a good sign, a sign that they are thinking seriously about this topic.
Finding Your Place in the Body	Once each member of the group has identified certain gifts, the question is how each one can get involved so that they are using their gifts to build the kingdom.
Mentoring Others	Finally, whether this is an initial session of learning about gifts involving the whole church, or a follow-up session for new members, each member needs to learn how to mentor others and pass on skills. This is what it means to "disciple" someone.

Introducing Spiritual Gifts

Small group leaders should do some study in preparation for leading this class or group. First, they should, at a minimum, study the scriptures listed below. Second, they should read the entire book and do the exercises as far as they are possible for an individual so they will know how one portion of the program relates to the next.

It is critical to keep our focus. Spiritual gifts is such a broad topic that it is easy to get distracted. Thus it is important to delay certain questions until the appropriate time when group members have the necessary background information.

Overview

The Bible doesn't have any section that presents spiritual gifts in an organized way. Even 1 Corinthians 12-14, which provides us with the most information we have, simply assumes the gifts and uses them as an illustration of how God has brought different elements together and brought them into unity for a single purpose under the one Spirit.

So, as we do in much of scripture, we are left to learn from experience, and the experience of the church in Corinth is a wonderful aid. Of course, that is not the only place we learn about gifts, but it is one of the most important.

This section discusses the basics of the baptism of the Holy Spirit and spiritual gifts. If you haven't studied the scriptures listed below, you should consider doing so before continuing in this passage, especially if you are leading the group study. There will be more things on which various churches and denominations disagree in this section than in any other portion of this study.

Scriptures

I suggest that your group consider studying the following scriptures in order to provide a good Biblical foundation for further learning. At a minimum, it would be a good idea to study the following scriptures:

1. 1 Corinthians 12-14
2. Ephesians 4:1-16
3. Romans 12:1-21
4. Acts (Study Outline available at http://www.deepbiblestudy.com/acts_outline.php)

I have included the basic outline of the Participatory Study Method and a worksheet to use if you wish to study those passages as a group. You can find more information at www.deepbiblestudy.com.

If your group has not studied them you might consider setting aside a few sessions to go look at this material before you continue with the study. This book will cover many things from these scriptures, but I always recommend going to the scriptures for yourself first.

There is a key to these passages. Each case in which the Paul presents the gifts is part of a discussion of unity. The gifts are to be under the control of one spirit and exercised by the body. I will discuss this in much more detail in a later lesson. For now, let me just say that this is why I emphasize so strongly using this course in the context of a church congregation. If you discover your gifts, but don't find a place of service as part of a Christian community, you are not just wasting your time. You're feeding your own pride.

It's all about working under the control of the Holy Spirit as part of the body of Jesus.

The Holy Spirit and Spiritual Gifts

What are spiritual gifts? Believe it or not, this is an area of some controversy in the church. I do not intend to settle all the debates in this book. That would be quite a daunting task. I am providing the information in the following chapter so that you can discuss in your group just what it is you and your church congregation believe about spiritual gifts. This is essential before you try to discover what gifts you have.

Receiving Spiritual Gifts

The baptism of the Holy Spirit is a controversial subject. Many Christians believe that there is only one experience of baptism, and that is when one comes to Christ. At that point one receives all of the Holy Spirit that one will receive, including whatever gifts of the Spirit God intends one to have. Charismatic and Pentecostal believers hold that there is a later experience of the baptism of the Holy Spirit at which one receives *gifts* of the Spirit. Some believe that this baptism must be accompanied by speaking in tongues.

Others believe that God gives the gifts at various times and places for specific uses. Thus one could experience the gift of healing when praying that someone will be healed, then lay hands on that person and heal them, but not possess the gift of healing. In other words, the gifts are not given to us to have and use at any time, but rather are given to us as needed according to our circumstances.

In using this book, it doesn't matter what your view on these issues is, except that if you don't believe that all of the gifts of the Spirit are still available in the church today, some of the questions on the survey will appear irrelevant. In the following material I will express my own view of the baptism of the Holy Spirit and how we receive and steward spiritual gifts to provide a foundation for the activities in this book. In your discussion time, you should compare this to your own church's statement on gifts, if you have one.

I believe that one cannot receive Christ apart from the work of the Holy Spirit and thus does receive the Holy Spirit in this sense when he or she accepts Jesus as savior. The ideal would be for us to teach clearly about the Holy Spirit when we accept new believers into membership and thus we could see the salvation and baptism in the Holy Spirit occur right at the beginning.

At the same time, the Christian life is one of growth, and one can have many further experiences with the Holy Spirit. The fact is that many Christians live without an awareness of the power of God that is available to them. They need to come to know the power of the Holy Spirit.

So what is the baptism of the Holy Spirit? It is the immersion of a Christian in the full power of the Holy Spirit, empowering that person for mission. In this book, *Baptism of the Holy Spirit* refers to any time of empowerment by the Holy Spirit and not to a singular event in a believer's life.

At the time of Pentecost (Acts 2:1-4) the disciples were together in one place waiting and praying. In later instances in the New Testament church, the Holy Spirit was received when the apostles prayed for people and laid hands on them. In Acts 10, however, there is no indication that Peter laid hands on the people for whom he prayed. It appears that those in the audience received the gift of the Holy Spirit while Peter was speaking.

Some examples of receiving the Holy Spirit are: John 20:22, Acts 2, Acts 8:4-25, Acts 10, and Acts 19:1-7.

The gift of the Holy Spirit is given to enable and empower God's people for mission and ministry. The basic pattern is found in Acts 2. The Spirit is given (verses 1-4) and then powerful ministry follows (verses 5 and following).

Trying to get the Holy Spirit in the wrong way, such as by buying the gift, or for the wrong purpose can be extremely dangerous. (See Acts 8:4-25).

> *But it is the Spirit who does all this and decides which gifts to give to each of us. – 1 Corinthians 12:11)*

The reception of one or more of the gifts of the Holy Spirit makes the internal, spiritual work of the Holy Spirit apparent in the life of the believer.

Is speaking in tongues the only sure sign of the Baptism of the Holy Spirit? I don't believe so. I believe that there must be a gift of the Spirit which shows the Holy Spirit at work in the believer's life. In the New Testament the gift of tongues almost always accompanies those cases in which the baptism is explicitly described. In many, even most, cases, the gift of tongues will accompany the Baptism of the Holy Spirit. In my own experience, the initial experience of the gift of the Holy Spirit is commonly, though not always, accompanied by the reception of a prayer language.*

Nonetheless in describing the gifts and how they are given, Paul indicates that not everyone will receive any specific gift (1 Corinthians

---

* A "prayer language" refers to the language one uses when praying in tongues, often seen either as an angelic language, or a spirit-language used in speaking to God. This must be distinguished from speaking in a known foreign language.

12:30) and that the Holy Spirit gives out the gifts as He decides (1 Corinthians 12:11).

The best indication that one is filled with the Holy Spirit is that one uses whatever gifts of the Holy Spirit one has to carry out the gospel commission (Matthew 28:18-20). The fruit is a better indicator than the gifts themselves.

Do not pressure people to receive the Holy Spirit, but always encourage them to take hold of everything that God offers them to aid in their Christian life. We should trust the Holy Spirit to work in each person's life in whatever way God ordains.

Paul told the jailer at Philippi: "Have faith in the Lord Jesus and you will be saved!" (Acts 16:31). For some people this is enough, and they are fearful to take the next step. But to be obedient to the Lord, one must also engage in ministry. Why would one refuse the power God offers to engage in ministry?

Gifts of the Holy Spirit

Paul lists the gifts in 1 Corinthians 12:8-11 and 12: 28-31 as:

- ✓ Words of Wisdom and Knowledge
- ✓ Faith, Healing, Miracles
- ✓ Prophecy
- ✓ Discerning spirits
- ✓ Speaking in tongues
- ✓ Interpreting tongues
- ✓ Leading and Helping

In addition, God has called various members of the body to different offices in service. The gifts and the offices are different, even when they relate to the same activity. A gift equips for a ministry; an office is that ministry in the church. For example, one can have the gift of prophecy while not exercising the office of prophet in the church.

Holiness

The book of Hebrews describes the requirements for the priests to approach God and then calls for us to approach God boldly through Jesus Christ.

> *"So let's come near God with pure hearts and a confidence that comes from having faith. Let's keep our hearts pure, and our consciences free from evil, and our bodies washed with clean water." – Hebrews 10:22*

When we experience the Holy Spirit we experience the presence of God. Jesus told his disciples that this was even better than his physical presence (John 16:7).

Gifts and Offices

> *Use good sense and measure yourself by the amount of faith that God has given you. A body is made up of many parts, and each of them has its own use. – Romans 12:3b-4*

This is a brief overview of gifts and offices. I will discuss them in more detail later in this chapter.

Distinguishing Fruit, Gifts, and Offices

The fruit of the Spirit is the manifestation of the character of Jesus in your own life through the indwelling and power of the Holy Spirit. The gifts of the Spirit are the ways in which God empowers a believer through the Holy Spirit to carry out ministry. The offices are simply ways in which God's power is used in the church body.

Gifts

There are a number of lists of gifts and offices in the Bible, including Romans 12:6-8, 1 Corinthians 12:7-11, and Ephesians 4:11-13. Many interpreters try to combine these lists to come up with a master list of the gifts, sometimes even deriving gifts from the offices. For example, the gift of "apostleship" is derived from the office of apostle.

The fact that the Bible provides different lists suggests that these lists are not intended to be exhaustive. In addition, the presence of God's Spirit accomplishes other things. For example, when the Spirit of God came on Samson, he killed a thousand of Israel's enemies (Judges 15).

So: A gift of the Spirit is any way in which God gives an individual power to carry out God's work.

They are:

✓ God's provision of an ability

✓ God's enabling for ministry

✓ God's manifestation of his power in the body of Christ

Because of this:

✓ Don't limit gifts to those listed in scripture; modern churches need gifts for handling the sound system, music, and construction, for example.

✓ Don't **eliminate** any gifts

Offices

The five offices listed in the Bible are apostles, prophet, evangelist, pastor and teacher. These are often called the "five-fold" ministries of the church. Most churches only recognize the last three of these offices, and many recognize only pastor and teacher. In turn, this often effectively gets reduced to just pastors.

As with the gifts, the people God has called into service do not always clearly fit one or another of these offices. Sometimes a person will combine aspects of more than one office in their ministry.

Some characteristics that identify a church office are:

- ✔ The way in which you use your gifts in the church
- ✔ Combinations of calling and gifts

Because of this:

- ✔ Many times a person's calling and gifts may not fit a single title
- ✔ Many times someone who holds a church office won't need a title—they will just do what needs to be done!
- ✔ Don't limit the offices to just those named in scripture
- ✔ Don't **eliminate** any of the offices named scripture.

Continuation of the Gifts and Offices

The common passage cited for this claim is 1 Corinthians 13:8-10. This passage tells us about the difference between our activity now under the guidance of the Spirit guided by the principle of love. Now we are always less than perfect. Our knowledge, even when we are inspired by God is incomplete. But a time will come when we will be with God in the kingdom of heaven and we will no longer need gifts of the Spirit. The time for ministry will be past. The "perfect" that Paul is speaking of in 1 Corinthians 13 is being in God's kingdom.

There is no statement in scripture that even suggests that any of the gifts of the Spirit are only temporary as long as we are in this world. ***All*** gifts are temporary to be replaced by God's presence when we are in God's eternal kingdom.

Apostles' Witness to Jesus

One rule for determining who was an apostle used in the early church was that the person in question had to have been a witness to Jesus and his ministry on earth. That is certainly a good way to distinguish the original apostles from their successors, but applying that rule in the same fashion to New Testament times, Paul couldn't be an apostle either. He saw Jesus after the ascension. God's power is not so limited that people cannot have visions of the risen Jesus today, just as they could in Paul's day. The 2,000 years since the time of Paul have not weakened God's power.

Yet the function of apostolic ministry continued in the church. I believe there have been people throughout the history of the church who have been called to an apostolic role, whether they have been known by that title or not.

A modern apostle may not add to scripture, and may not give witness to the physical life of Jesus. But he should lead the church as an apostle, and should bear witness to the presence of Jesus in his own life and ministry.

Apostles are important to the church in that they direct and guide evangelistic efforts and exercise authority beyond our normal boundaries. The church would do well to try to recognize those who exercise apostolic authority and allow those people to operate across denominational boundaries.

Using the Gifts and Offices

Just as the gifts and offices are given by God, so they are exercised under God's power.

> *Christ chose…so that his people would learn to serve and his body would grow strong. This will continue until we are united by our faith and by our understanding of the Son of God. – Ephesians 4:11-13*

Discussion of the Biblical Gifts

The following section provides a discussion of the major gifts listed in the Bible. Earlier, I claimed that there are many more gifts that God would like to give, and even that were manifested in Biblical times. The key to determining whether a gift is given by the Spirit of God is that it will be under the control of the one Spirit. Any Spirit that denies Jesus is not of God.

Prophecy

Speaking for God

Prophecy is speaking the word or message of God for a particular circumstance or time.

In Biblical times prophets foretold the future, condemned unrighteous acts, gave encouragement, recommended courses of action to rulers or to priests and warned of judgment.

Only a small portion of the work of a prophet involves predicting the future, and even the predictions are designed either to teach or to correct.

The Gift of Prophecy

The gift of prophecy is the gift of receiving messages from the Lord to speak forth for others. These messages can come at any time or place and are often not under the conscious control of the person who speaks them so that the person speaking does not choose whether to utter the message. (If the gift of prophecy is true, the message will always be from God, of course.)

The gift of prophecy is one of the gifts through which we get information given by the Holy Spirit for the church. Others are words of knowledge or wisdom and discernment. Prophecy is distinguished from these other gifts in that it provides a direct message from God and is usually identified as the word of the Lord when the prophet speaks it in one way or another, though not always.

A person with the gift of prophecy may receive messages in various ways other than the spoken word, including visions (Ezekiel 1), dreams (Daniel 7), words of knowledge or wisdom, discernment and the operation of another spiritual gift such as teaching (Paul's epistles, Hebrews, James). Very often the prophet's message will come in a way that requires the prophet to find the words to describe the message. It may even be in the form of a strong emotional impression.

Prophetic Gift and Office

The gift of prophecy and the office of a prophet are different. Many people may have the gift of prophecy to use in whatever office they exercise in the church. A pastor, evangelist or teacher may have this gift. An apostle probably will have it.

The office of the prophet is one established in the church to provide continuing correction and guidance from a person that the church recognizes as possessing a true gift. The church also recognizes that the person is reliable in the exercise of that gift and has the wisdom to use it properly. In appointing someone to the office of prophet, the church recognizes that the person so commissioned will speak the word of the Lord only when he or she is certain that a message is from God.

Pastors, evangelists, teachers and other church leaders, as well as those exercising the office of the prophet must apply discernment to any message identified as a word from the Lord, and must correct those who express a false word.

Presentation of Prophecy

Prophecy does not come in a special vocabulary or form. It may come in educated speech or in uneducated. It will be framed in words appropriate to the personality of the person expressing the message. Often people exercising the prophetic gift try to use theological wording, Biblical phrases or even archaic language to express the prophecy. It is alright to express a message you have received from God in ordinary speech.

In receiving the Word of the Lord, we must separate the way the message is delivered from the message itself. God has always used a variety of messengers and methods to present His word.

Don't let the speaker, writer or the form in which the message comes distract you from the message.

Testing Prophetic Utterances

We are instructed to test the spirits to see whether they are of God. In Deuteronomy 18:21-22 we are told that if God says something will happen, then it will happen. This is a way to test the word of a prophet. But we must modify this test with the words of Jeremiah (chapter 18) and the example of Jonah in which the predicted event does not take place. But it does not take place for a reason-because the word accomplished its goal of correction. The word accomplishes what God intended it to accomplish, even if it does not accomplish what we think it should.

Deuteronomy 13:1-5 provides another test that is easier to apply. If the prophet tells us to worship other gods, his message is not true.

This test can be applied before one waits for the fulfillment of any prediction. It even applies to prophecies that do not contain predictions.

The Gift of Prophecy and Scripture

Both the message of someone exercising the gift of prophecy and the Bible bring us the word of the Lord. In the case of the Bible, however, we have a word that has stood the test of years of use by God's people and has been accepted of the church, guided by the Holy Spirit.

The Word as revealed in scripture is thus the standard by which other words are judged. Unlike Abraham, we have the benefit of both the scriptures and the tradition of the church by which to judge our own individual experiences.

Dangers of Prophecy

The penalty for false prophecy in Biblical times was death (Deuteronomy 18:20). While we don't have the death penalty in church life today, one should always be careful when claiming that something is a word from the Lord. God's name is not to be taken carelessly or lightly.

Pastors and other leaders must use discernment in dealing with those who claim a word from the Lord.

Speaking in Tongues

> *What if I could speak all languages of humans and of angels? If I did not love others, I would be nothing more than a noisy gong or a clanging cymbal. – 1 Corinthians 13:1*

What are 'Tongues'?

There are differences of opinion as to precisely what the gift of tongues is. Some believe it is only speaking in foreign languages for purposes of evangelism. This is the manifestation that occurred on the day of Pentecost (Acts 2). Others believe that there is a spiritual prayer language that each person receives when they are baptized in (or into) the Holy Spirit, and that this is separate from a gift of speaking in foreign languages. In 1 Corinthians 14, when Paul discusses church order, he seems to be speaking about this type of prayer language, and also of a type of language that can be interpreted as a person speaks God's word. This may be the "tongues of angels" to which he referred earlier in 1 Corinthians 13.

Because there are scriptures that speak of both kinds of activity, and because the precise definition of "speaking in tongues" is controversial, it is a good idea to be gentle, patient and tolerant in using and speaking about this gift, or in restricting its use. Love and unity is more important.

A person's prayer language is very precious, and allows an expression of the heart to God without intervention of our limited understanding. This has value in itself. Rejoice at the freedom God has given you for prayer, but always be aware of church order and the unity of the Body (see below).

Tongues and Interpretation

The key question in Paul's first letter to the Corinthians was "What is it that makes somebody spiritual?" Some thought it was the person who had brought them the gospel, some thought it was their freedom and rights, others thought it was their gifts.

In 1 Corinthians 12, Paul outlines the various gifts and shows how they must work together. God brings different gifts together in the Body to make a whole body with all the abilities needed to accomplish His work. In chapter 13, Paul tells us that the prime consideration in everything that we do in ministry is how it relates to love. In chapter 14 he discusses our spiritual gifts in relation to meeting for worship.

Using the Gifts as a Body

Paul tells us that we can control the way we behave, and that we need to do so in order to provide a good witness. He is concerned that the use of spiritual gifts in the worship service both serve to build up the church, and also serve as a witness to others (1 Corinthians 14:23).

> *My friends, when you meet to worship, you must do everything for the good of everyone there. That's how it should be when someone sings or teaches or tells what God has said or speaks an unknown language or explains what the language means.*
> *- 1 Corinthians 14:26*

Many wonder what Paul means by "decently and in order" (verse 40). But he has already defined it: Whatever builds the entire Church is done decently and in order.

In many modern churches, we take this command as a restriction on many things that the Corinthian church probably never even imagined. Before building rules for your church from 1 Corinthians 14, try to imagine the service that brought forth Paul's criticism. It was clearly a raucous time, with multiple people speaking in tongues at the same time, or prophesying, with no order and control. It was that situation that Paul sought to correct.

Tongues and Prayer Ministry

When we pray for others during altar prayer time, or any time when they hear what we are saying in prayer, we must remember that we are not only conversing with God. They are a part of the conversation. We need to consider what kind of a witness our words and actions will be. In addition, if we are working with other people in prayer ministry, we must make sure that we work in unity.

Praying in tongues can be a great blessing, and if the person being prayed for and those on the ministry team understand and can be in unity in that prayer, then go ahead. But if there is any question about either the witness or unity, then pray in plain language. Someone who doesn't understand what you are doing could be confused or driven away. It is all about bringing the one needing ministry closer to Jesus.

> *In certain ways we are weak, but the Spirit is here to help us. For example, when we don't know what to pray for, the Spirit prays for us in ways that cannot be put into words. All of our thoughts are known to God. He can understand what is in the mind of the Spirit, as the Spirit prays for God's people. – Romans 8:26-27*

Leadership

Biblical Leaders

Much of the Bible is in the form of stories. We often spend our time trying to figure out details of theological portions of the Bible while the clear explanation is easily available in the form of stories.

Leadership is like that. You will find only a few lists of characteristics that God expects his leaders to display. But in the stories you will find people that God called into leadership and evaluations of what they did. Learn from the example of God's leaders.

Moses - His call is related in Exodus 3 & 4. Moses didn't want to go, but when God insisted and even became angry he did. God first equipped Moses with a helper (his brother Aaron) but as time went on, Moses grew in his own gifts.

Deborah - We don't know how Deborah was equipped, but we do know that it must have been a divine call for her to lead as a judge in a day when women just didn't take such positions. In the end, she went to battle with a general who wouldn't go unless she went along (Judges 4 & 5).

Gideon - Gideon was hiding out threshing wheat in a wine press so he wouldn't be found. God held Gideon's hand by giving him signs as he learned to obey and trust God (Judges 7 & 8).

Mary - While an angel delivered the call of God, Mary seems to have been equipped from the very start. Unlike many who argued, she said, "I am the Lord's servant! Let it happen as you have said" (Luke 1:38). That is a truly extraordinary response to the initial call of God to a difficult mission.

Peter - Peter was an impetuous fisherman. Jesus equipped him through three and a half years of teaching, then the trials of the crucifixion, and finally through the outpouring of God's power at Pentecost.

Paul - God had to knock Paul down on the ground and strike him blind to get his attention. Once he was called, however, he was equipped through the gifts of the Spirit, and also experience. In reading Paul's letters in the New Testament, we can watch him grow in his call.

Key Passages

If there are questions in your group about leadership, try studying some of these passages. Romans 12, 1 Corinthians 12, and Ephesians 4 are particularly applicable to this study.

Romans 12 - deals with authority, how the body works together, spiritual gifts, and ties it all together in service.

1 Corinthians 12 - lists the gifts of the Spirit, but more importantly tells us how the various gifts work together in one body, subject to the rule of love (1 Corinthians 13).

Ephesians, 1 Timothy, Titus - these are the more technical and pastoral letters that explain something about how leadership is exercised in the church.

Leadership Prerequisites

There really is only one: ***Be willing!***

Read Hebrews 11 some time and look up each person's name in a concordance. How many were prepared for service when they were called? God can use anyone, even a donkey, to lead someone!

Here are the key prerequisites for leadership in the body:

- ✔ Willingness
- ✔ Grace - God's gift
- ✔ Love for God
- ✔ Love for one another
- ✔ Utilize wisely the resources God has provided

Leaders and Followers

Every Christian is in a position to lead, however small or obscure that position, even if you only lead through your witness for Christ. Some people are called to lead more people, and to lead in more ways than others are, and we tend to call these people leaders. God also requires followers, and good leaders are often good followers.

Leadership is not always about acting or speaking. If God gave you the vision for an event or activity, you were obedient, and God's vision is being carried out, you are a leader whether or not you appear to be leading, and whether or not you get the credit.

> *Don't be jealous or proud, but be humble and consider others more important than yourselves. Care about them as much as you care about yourselves and think the same way that Christ Jesus thought. – Philippians 2:3-5 CEV*

Helping

God made promises to us that He would not leave us or forsake us and that He would help us, His children. Yes, He can reach down and personally give me whatever help I need but it is His plan to mold us into a 'body' that functions in harmony and helps each other. Some are especially gifted in the area of helping.

Who are some of the "helpers" in the Bible?

- Aaron (Exodus 7) gifted to speak for Moses to Pharaoh
- Hur (Exodus 17) helped hold Moses arms up - battle was won
- Bezalel (Exodus 31, 35, 36) helped Moses, gifted by God as a craftsman
- Stephen and 6 others (Acts 6) helped distribute food among the widows
- Tabitha/Dorcas (Acts 9) helped the poor

What are some characteristics of someone with the 'gift of helps'?

- A 'servant heart' - it is a yearning to assist anyone in need
- 'Sight' to see needs in others – many times this is non-verbal, a discernment
- Able to recognize the needs of a leader sometimes before they know there is a need!
- Able to utilize the resources God has provided (they can think "out of the box")

In the world, this person might be an outstanding administrative assistant, chairman of a charitable committee, or an organized, innovative homemaker. They might love to participate in outreach opportunities or mission trips or help cook Wednesday night dinners. They nurture and nourish the individuals of the church with their ability to see the needs of the one and the needs of groups.

Is "helping" done under the anointing of the Holy Spirit?

Our tendency is to think of spectacular things coming from the Holy Spirit, and more ordinary things coming from ourselves. But the fact is that all gifts come from God.

> *Every good and perfect gift comes down from the Father who created all the lights in the heavens. – James 1:17*

When we see someone in the church speaking in tongues, or praying for someone and they are healed, or preaching an exceptional sermon, we think of them as gifted. But the Holy Spirit is just as much involved when someone knows how to see the things that need to be done, how to go about helping, and is willing to do what is needed.

A friend of mine who is a pastor calls these "two by four" ministries, because, like the frame of a house, they are covered up by the more spectacular things, but they are absolutely essential. God wants us to see through to the hidden, helping ministries.

> *First, God chose some people to be apostles and prophets and teachers for the church. But he also chose some to work miracles or heal the sick or help others or be leaders or speak different kinds of languages. – 1 Corinthians 12:28*

Leadership and Helping

As we work together in the body everybody will have some opportunities to lead, and everyone will have some opportunities to follow. Often these will both happen at the same time.

The person who can follow the best will often be the best type of leader. Jesus chose 12 men to be disciples-that is people who would follow him and learn from him. When it was all done, they were called apostles-people who were sent forth to do a mission. They were God's helpers!

But to the church they were leaders, "pastors to the pastors" of the various churches, teaching and even defining new doctrine for the young church. There are no leaders in the kingdom who were not at some time good followers.

Encouragement

> *A body is made up of many parts, and each of them has its own use. That's how it is with us. There are many of us, but we each are part of the body of Christ, as well as part of one another. . . . If we can encourage others, we should encourage them. – Romans 12:4-5, 8*

Encouragement and Exhortation

In the New Testament, encouragement and exhortation are part of the same thing, and often are used to translate the same Greek word.

A person who has the gift of encouragement will generally:

- ✔ Know when someone is in need, even when they are not present.
- ✔ Be able to respond to someone else's need in a caring and appropriate manner.
- ✔ Present both encouragement and rebuke as necessary, and do so with grace.
- ✔ Have a way of providing encouragement that is unique and fits their own personality and experience.

Rebuke and Encouragement

Generally, those with the gift of encouragement don't want to offer rebuke, but they will also be obedient to the Holy Spirit when they are called upon to do so. Prophets very often rebuke, and sometimes do so harshly, often because a harsh rebuke is needed. But encouragers can provide the rebuke in a much gentler manner and do so with exceptional grace, precisely because they don't want to do it. Much heartache can be prevented by a grace-filled suggestions offered before the need comes for harder words.

As with all the gifts of the Spirit, listening to the Holy Spirit and acting when, and only when the Holy Spirit directs is important.

Be very careful, however, if you feel called to rebuke, that you are not simply being critical and following your own agenda.

Encouragement in the Church

Encouragement is a simple gift in the church. There is rarely any objection to speaking encouragement to people, to sending them cards or letters, or simply presenting a positive attitude.

The seemingly little things that encouragers do have a much more serious impact than the individual church member is likely to recognize.

Encouragers quite often don't recognize their gift, because it is easy to exercise naturally, and others don't speak about it as often. But this gift is critical to the church. Your church will run much more smoothly if it is recognized and encouraged.

The Example of Biblical Encouragers

Joseph – This young man learned the need for encouragement by the way he grew up. He was not an encourager until God disciplined him into becoming one. We see examples of his encouragement in Genesis

49:19-21 when he not only forgave his brothers, but encouraged them. Then he provides encouragement to the whole people of Israel by telling them to take his body from Egypt back to Canaan when God leads them out. This unusual method of encouragement should remind us that God can use encouragers in unusual ways.

Aaron and Hur – Aaron and Hur held up the Moses' arms during battle (Exodus 17:8-16). This story reminds us that an encourager needs to know when he or she cannot do the task, but that God has anointed someone else, and it is time to get behind the one God has anointed. Aaron and Hur could have thought **they** should hold up **their** own hands, but they recognized that God had anointed Moses as the leader, and they got behind him.

Peter – On the day of Pentecost, this apostle proclaimed the resurrection of Jesus and 3,000 people believed. This is one of the most commonly recognized forms of encouragement or exhortation—preaching. While preaching is just one of the many ways people can be encouraged or exhorted, it is still extremely important.

Jesus – Read Luke 22:31-34 where Jesus encourages Peter, tells him he has prayed for him, and expresses confidence in the result.

> *My friends, watch out! Don't let evil thoughts or doubts make any of you turn from the living God. You must encourage one another each day. – Hebrews 3:12-13*

Healing

> *When Jesus got out of the boat, he saw the large crowd. He felt sorry for them and healed everyone who was sick. – Matthew 14:14*

The Bible has a great deal to say about healing, though it is mostly in the form of stories. God's idea of healing is to restore us spiritually, mentally, and physically.

I hope that you are as strong in body, as I know you are in spirit. – 3 John 2a

We sometimes err when we put our focus on physical healing ahead of spiritual health and healing, or when we see physical health as our primary goal. We also err, however, if we believe that God does not care about physical healing or cannot heal physically.

He was wounded and crushed
because of our sins;
by taking our punishment,
He made us completely well. – Isaiah 53:5

We should notice here that the key issue is our sins, the things that separate us from God. That is God's first concern. Often, physical healing will follow spiritual and emotional healing.

Don't let <u>your</u> agenda get in the way of God following <u>His</u> path to healing!

God placed healing above other activities. He was willing to heal on the Sabbath (John 7). Ultimately healing means the conquering of death (John 11), and all the glory goes to God.

God granted gifts of healing to the church (1 Corinthians 12:9), and this should be the key to our ministry. (See Acts 3 and the story of Peter healing the lame man.) Do we have less power in the church, especially for healing, because we have more silver and gold?

Why doesn't everyone get healed when I pray?

There can be many reasons why physical healing does not take place. First we must consider God's will. People prefer to think that God will heal everyone physically here and now, but sometimes God is ready to take people home.

For other possibilities, see our Energion Publications pamphlet, "I Want to be Healed!"

Healing Prayer and Professional Medicine

There should be no territorial wall between the medical profession and the healing ministry of the church. God chooses to work through multiple means, some of which we call "natural" and some we call "supernatural" but that is a distinction that God doesn't make. It's all just natural to him!

There is nothing about prayer, anointing, and laying hands on people that will prevent pursuing the best medical care possible. Seeking the best medical care is not a sign that you lack faith; rather, it is a sign that you are seeking healing through every means that God has made available.

Those who pray for the sick should encourage people to cooperate with God through healthy living and by following sound medical advice. God does not expect you to turn away any of the gifts he has given.

> *The angel showed me a river that was crystal clear, and its waters gave life...On each side of the river are trees that grow a different kind of fruit each month of the year. The fruit give life, and the leaves are used as medicine to heal the nations. – Revelation 22:1,2*

Knowledge and Wisdom

> *If any of you need wisdom, you should ask God, and it will be given to you. God is generous and won't correct you for asking. – James 1:5*

Word

Some interpreters hold that this refers to a single word, and identify such single words as "words of knowledge" or "words of wisdom" but the Greek word here "logos" can mean message as well.

The distinction between these gifts and prophecy is not in the number of words or the amount of information, but in the circumstances.

A **word of knowledge** is a message that provides particular information that is needed by the church body at a particular time. It may provide direction in ministry, or it may provide information on possible traps or danger.

A **word of wisdom** brings together knowledge that already exists and gives direction in its proper use. Just because we know certain things doesn't mean we will use them in the best possible way. Especially in committees and groups we can become focused on a course of action, and no matter what problems or alternatives are suggested, people may be set on a particular path. A word of wisdom, spoken properly, can restore clear vision and good sense.

Words and Prophecy

While many Christians treat prophecy as though it was a source of information to satisfy their curiosity about the future, that is not its primary purpose. Prophecy gives a message about God's will or his intentions. That word can be corrective as in a rebuke or encouraging. It may give information about the present or the future, but the information it gives is intended to direct our actions.

A word or message of knowledge, on the other hand is just that! It gives us information, and we can choose to do what we want with that information.

Some examples of messages of knowledge include:

✓ Direction to the prayer team leader as to who will fit well to minister to each person, and how that prayer may need to proceed.

✓ Information on a person in need in the congregation, sometimes for healing, sometimes for salvation.

✓ Information that there is a need to be met at a particular time and place, even during worship.

Sometimes God will speak in unexpected ways. Don't limit the functioning of this gift by failing to recognize when God is speaking because you are not accustomed to the method.

Wisdom and a Word of Wisdom

Wisdom is one of the few things that God has promised absolutely if we ask in faith (James 1:5).

A word of wisdom is not different from wisdom in general except that it comes supernaturally at a critical moment. A word of wisdom sometimes makes up for a failure of wisdom, but it also makes up sometimes for things that we could not possibly foresee.

Using Words of Knowledge and Wisdom

These gifts should be used in the same way as any other gifts. You need to listen to the Holy Spirit and use the gifts to build up the body. This means working with cooperation between leadership and laity.

Discernment should be applied in the same way as with prophecy. We always need to decide whether something is a word from God or comes from a person's own agenda. When something is from God we need to follow God's command, or take action based on the information we have. If something is not from God, we need to be aware of it, and sometimes to speak a word of rebuke.

To one is given through the Spirit the utterance of wisdom, and to another the utterance of knowledge according to the same Spirit. – 1 Corinthians 12:8 (NRSV)

Miracles

So if we refuse this great way of being saved, how can we hope to escape? The Lord himself was the first to tell about it, and people who heard the message proved to us that it was true. God himself showed that his message was true by working all kinds of powerful miracles and wonders. He also gave his Holy Spirit to anyone he chose to. – Hebrews 2:3-4

A miracle is anything that God does in the world that is out of the ordinary. We sometimes have trouble identifying miracles because they are always unexpected.

The Purpose of Miracles

God performs miracles (sometimes called signs and wonders) to get our attention, to teach us lessons, and to confirm his word.

It is possible to see a miracle and miss the point entirely. The people who ate the food that Jesus provided to the 5,000 certainly saw a miracle take place, and they identified who had done it. But they missed the point.

The Gift of Miracles

God can perform a miracle as the result of anyone's prayer, but there are some people who are given a special anointing or gift of performing miracles so that they can carry out their calling. These people will see extraordinary things happen as they minister.

Miracles and the Gospel Message

When Peter spoke on the day of Pentecost, he said:

> *Now, listen to what I have to say about Jesus from Nazareth. God proved that he sent Jesus to you by having him work miracles, wonders, and signs. All of you know this. – Acts 2:22*

The signs help to confirm the gospel message. We cannot be sure that something that appears wonderful to us is a sign of God's favor. In Deuteronomy we are told that even if a prophet gives a sign, and that sign is fulfilled, and then he tells us to worship other gods we should not follow. But the combination of God's message with confirmation by signs and wonders is a signature of God's activity.

Miracles Today

Each believer must use discernment in listening to miracle claims. People can easily claim miracles. But the early disciples continued with this power, it was promised to the church, and it continues in the church today.

Be careful that you look at what God is pointing you to. The miracle is a sign—it points you to God. If you see only the miraculous event and do not lift your eyes to see God and his message, it's just an exciting event.

Anyone who has the gift of miracles should be careful to give God the credit, just as the early disciples did. It is not you, but God, who is working. It is not your agenda, but God's, that must be followed.

The meaning of some Biblical Miracles

Elijah – brought down fire from heaven. This was not to show simply that God could bring down fire, but rather to point the Israelites to the one true God.

Water to wine – shows that God is interested in the little joys of life, but also symbolized the new spiritual wine that Jesus was about to pour out for his people.

Healing of the man born blind – shows God's healing power, but also illustrates spiritual blindness, and how Jesus is willing to open our spiritual eyes.

Raising of Lazarus – shows Jesus as the Lord not only of life, but of death. Mary and Martha thought that Jesus could only save Lazarus if he was present before death. Jesus showed that his power was not so limited.

Resurrection of Jesus – tells us that Satan's power is broken forever. Our salvation is the GREATEST miracle of all!

> *Jesus answered, "I tell you for certain that you are not looking for me because you saw the miracles, but because you ate all the food you wanted. Don't work for food that spoils. Work for food that gives eternal life. The Son of Man will give you this food, because God the Father has given him the right to do so."*
>
> *"What exactly does God want us to do?" the people asked.*
>
> *Jesus answered, "God wants you to have faith in the one he sent." – John 6:26-29*

Questions and Exercises

In the chapters that follow you will have an opportunity to discuss your own spiritual gifts and those of others in the group. For this chapter, try to keep the discussion generic and impersonal. Know the boundaries of your church body. I do not mean to suggest that a church can override God's word on a subject, but while you are a member of a church congregation, you should live up to the standards of that organization. The gifts are given as needed in the body of Christ, and must be used cooperatively, not competitively.

1. Does your church have a doctrinal statement on the baptism of the Holy Spirit? What do you believe, and why?

---

2. Does your church have a doctrinal statement on the gifts of the Spirit?

---

3. Do any of these spiritual gifts make you uncomfortable? Why?

4. What spiritual gifts do you find most interesting?

Spirit Led Ministry

You should study this section with two questions in mind:

1) How can *you* find a place of ministry in the church?
2) How can you *help others* to find their own place of ministry?

You will find the answers to these questions in the way the church is led.

Most Christians see the major issue with spiritual gifts as one of how many gifts we use and when and where we use them. But Paul, in 1 Corinthians 12, makes it very clear that the issue is one of **who is leading** us.

> *You know that when you were still pagans you were led astray and swept along in worshiping speechless idols. – 1 Corinthians 12:2 (NLT)*

Thus the key element of paganism here is that individuals are led in various directions according to the various spirits that the individuals choose to follow. The problem in the Corinthian church was that the people who had become Christians were still doing more or less the same things as they did before they became Christians. In 1 Corinthians 12-14 Paul repeatedly emphasized two points:

1. Everything is guided by one Spirit

2. Everything is done to build up the body

Paul states all of this in the verses that follow immediately. By contrast with Paganism, Paul calls for the church to bring its great variety of resources under the control of one Spirit.

> *[4]Now there are varieties of gifts, but the same Spirit; [5]and there are varieties of services, but the* ***same*** *Lord; [6]and there are varieties of activities, but it is the* ***same*** *God who* <u>*activates* ***all*** *of them in* ***everyone.***</u> *– 1 Corinthians 12:4-6 (NRSV, emphasis mine)*

So the church is characterized by great variety that is brought into unity as it brings itself into one Spirit.

It's important to notice at this point that everyone who receives Christ is brought under the power of this Spirit. It is not the result of a special event such as the baptism of the Holy Spirit (see page), but simply the result of putting our trust in Jesus Christ at salvation. When we put our trust in Jesus Christ he gives us his Spirit. As Paul says:

> *[12] For just as the body is one and has many members, and all the members of the body, though many, are one body, so it is with Christ. [13] For in the one Spirit we were all baptized into one body—Jews or Greeks, slaves or free—and we were all made to drink of one Spirit.*
> *– 1 Corinthians 12:12-13 (NRSV)*

The reason it is important to emphasize this point is that everyone in the church is gifted by God. There is no specially privileged group. There are only Christians, gifted by God, empowered and guided by the one Holy Spirit. The experience of Spirit baptism can bring new gifts to our awareness and help us to use them, but the Holy Spirit is active in all Christians.

Our natural response to the diversity that is present in any congregation is to attempt to control it. Control is characterized by the following:

- ✔ Limit the diversity of ministry
  Control results from fear and thus looks first at the safety of any sort of ministry. What harm can be done? How can we prevent such harm? If there is a potential for harm, then control hopes to prevent the danger by cutting off the ministry.

- ✔ Aims to prevent problems
  Rather than looking at the potential benefits of a ministry, a controller looks at managing the risk.

- ✔ Characterized by "emergency response" approach
  Often the person interested in control prefers to leave things alone and prefers to ignore them. This is not a desire for freedom, but rather an attempt to keep activities quiet so that they don't get out of hand. When they do get out of hand, then the emergency response is generally to clamp a large body of rules to prevent the potential risks.

In contrast the leading of the Spirit places emphasis on ministry.

- ✔ Brings diversity into the body
  Spirit led ministry tries to bring all parts of the body into full participation in the ministry of the church, because that is the way the body can best be built up.

- ✔ Guides the diversity into unity of ministry
  Unity of action using a diversity of people and diversity of gifts is the true mark of a Spirit led ministry

- ✔ Focuses on maximizing the ministry
  Spirit led ministry does not focus on giving particular people credit, or on minimizing the risks, but rather on maximizing the

ministry. (Note that maximizing the ministry may involve minimizing risks; the issue is which of the two is your primary focus.)

- ✔ Constantly anticipates needs
  Instead of waiting for trouble, Spirit led ministry is always looking for needs to fulfill.

- ✔ Brings maximum gifts to bear on each need
  Whatever gifts are available and relevant are brought to bear on the problem.

- ✔ 100% accurate
  This doesn't mean that we will never make mistakes. Our hearing is not always perfect, but God's speaking is. We need to practice listening.

Let's illustrate this with a situation in which the gift of prophecy is first encountered in a congregation. A desire for control suggests first that we try to keep it from becoming a major factor. If people only speak words of prophecy in private, at homes, or in the pastor's office, then the church as a whole is not threatened by it. If it can't be kept quiet we look for a series of rules. Now rules may be necessary, but rules that are enacted as a *response* to trouble will be aimed at protecting against potential problems, and not at maximizing the effectiveness of the gift..

A Spirit guided response will be asking first how this new gift manifested in the church can be used to build up the church. There will almost certainly still be rules for its exercise in the congregation, but it is very unlikely that these will involve keeping the gift secret or segregated. The rules will emphasize providing an opportunity for the church to benefit rather than simply protecting the leadership or the reputation of the church. Those with the gift of prophecy will not be seen as a privileged elite, nor as a dangerous force, but rather as just one element of the diversity that God has placed in the body.

Fruit and Gifts

Many people confuse the fruit of the Spirit and the gifts. More importantly they confuse the relationship between the two. It's very easy to get dazzled by the gifts and assume that the presence of powerful, visible, supernatural activity is the test of God's presence. But as we saw at the beginning of this chapter, a better test is that we all work together under the one Spirit. Another way to describe that ministry is by saying that it is carried out by people displaying the fruit of the Spirit.

As Paul describes it:

> 22 *God's Spirit makes us loving, happy, peaceful, patient, kind, good, faithful,* 23 *gentle, and self-controlled. There is no law against behaving in any of these ways.* 24 *And because we belong to Christ Jesus, we have killed our selfish feelings and desires.* 25 *God's Spirit has given us life, and so we should follow the Spirit.* 26 *But don't be conceited or make others jealous by claiming to be better than they are. – Galatians 5:22-26*

This describes the way people who are part of the body of Christ—those controlled by the one Spirit—are to behave. In effect, it is simply a restatement of the same thing. Note also the similarity to 1 Corinthians 13, in which Paul places love above all of the gifts of the Spirit. It's not merely that love is more important. Love is what gives our ministry its form, guidance, and meaning.

The fruit of the Spirit are an identifying characteristic of God's Spirit at work. This can be an aid in our discernment.

Fruit and gifts are similar in many ways:

- ✔ Both come from the same Spirit
  They will not be in conflict. If there is conflict you know that a wrong spirit is operating somewhere.
- ✔ Both are necessary for your ministry
  You can't just have one or the other. The tendency is to think that because the fruit are a visible, identifying trait that we're all right as long as we have the fruit. But a person can be truly loving, kind, nice, patient, and so forth and still be ineffective.
- ✔ Both must be exercised
  Neither the fruit nor the gifts are things that you kind of sit around and "have." They have to be used.
- ✔ Both are important
  We like to prioritize things, and that is often good. But in order to accomplish God's mission we are going to need both fruit and gifts. We can't work effectively if we're missing either one.

Here is a way to contrast the fruit and the gifts:

> Fruit is the way in which the Holy Spirit changes you.
>
> ---
>
> Gifts are the way in which the Spirit enables you to practice the fruit.

Fruit of the Spirit and Love	
Fruit (Galatians 5:22-23)	Love (1 Corinthians 13)
✔ Love ✔ Joy ✔ Peace ✔ Patience ✔ Kindness ✔ Generosity ✔ Faithfulness ✔ Gentleness ✔ Self-control	✔ Patient ✔ Kind ✔ Not envious, boastful, arrogant, or rude ✔ Does not insist on its own way ✔ Not irritable or resentful ✔ Does not rejoice in wrongdoing, but rejoices in the truth ✔ Bears, believes, hopes, endures all things (which means it is forgiving and doesn't make lists)

Talents and Gifts

Talents and gifts are often confused. Our talents are given to us at birth and are part of who we are. Whether we are filled with the Spirit or not, we can have talents. A person who is filled with the Spirit will make their talents into gifts simply by using them under the control of the Holy Spirit. I do not mean that talents are equivalent to gifts, nor that the gifts of the Spirit are simply our sanctified talents. What I mean is that our talents are also God's gift, and he asks us to use them in his service. God then makes everything he has given us *more than we can do*. He makes them *what God can do through each of us*.

The gifts of the Spirit add a supernatural element, whether the gift is one that seems mundane, like administration, or is one that seems spectacular, like prophecy. There is no scriptural basis to decide that the Spirit of God is less active in a gift that we don't think is as spectacular. The church is generally in need of many more administrators, encouragers, and helpers than prophets. We, on the other hand, would rather be prophets.

Personal Example:

To illustrate gifts and talents, I believe I have a talent for teaching. I was able to teach quite well when I was not part of the church and was certainly not in tune with the Holy Spirit. The talent for teaching was there all the time.

When I put that talent to work for God, it was still just a talent. I was good at what I was doing. But then there was the day that I stepped into a Sunday School class, carrying the notes for my well prepared *talented* lesson, and found that the class was stirred up about something else. Our church was experiencing the winds of revival, but the revival came from another church, and it came with activities and characteristics with which many of the class members were uncomfortable.

"You're not going to teach about Proverbs today," said one member. "You're going to talk about revival." He plunked down a stack of duplicated sheets in front of me that provided material from a number of commentaries. I didn't know what to do. I was prepared to talk about Proverbs, but nobody was prepared to listen.

I opened the class with prayer, still not knowing what I was going to say next. When I finished the prayer I heard myself say, "What do you think our church would look like if God brought revival?" Now understand that this is not a story to the credit of Henry Neufeld. When I say, "I heard myself say" I mean precisely that. I didn't produce that question. But it was the **right** question. The class began to answer it, and I took notes. I hardly talked throughout the session. At the end I simply read down the list and said, "Why don't we go home and pray for this in our church?"

There was a lesson taught that day, but it went beyond anything that my talent for teaching could possibly have produced. That was the day I first experienced the **gift** of teaching.

Gifts and Offices

The gifts of the Spirit and offices in the church are again often confused. There is a gift of teaching, but it is not identical to the office of teacher. There is a gift of apostleship, but it is not necessarily identical to having the office of apostle. There is a gift of prophecy, but it is not necessarily equivalent to having the office of prophet.

The two can be contrasted as follows:

Gifts and Offices Compared	
Gifts are:	Offices are:
✔ God's provision of an ability ✔ God's enabling for ministry ✔ God's manifestation of his power in the body of Christ ✔ Don't limit gifts to those listed in scripture (sound system, music, construction) ✔ Don't **eliminate** any gifts	✔ The way in which you use your gifts in the church ✔ Many times don't need to be named ✔ Don't limit them to the named offices in scripture ✔ Don't **eliminate** any named offices

I don't believe that the lists of gifts and offices in the Bible are intended as a limitation. Rather those lists just illustrate what God is willing to do. I also don't believe that God wants to force a single organizational structure on the church. The offices are again simply a starting point.

It is critical, however, that we don't start eliminating part of God's starting point, or the core elements of God's plan for ministry. We can have offices that combine various gifts in different ways, but we're always going to need the basic elements.

> [11] *The gifts he gave were that some would be apostles, some prophets, some evangelists, some pastors and teachers,* [12] *to equip the saints for the work of ministry, for building up the body of Christ,* [13] *until all of us come to the unity of the faith and of the knowledge of the Son of God, to maturity, to the measure of the full stature of Christ. – Ephesians 4:11-13 (NRSV, emphasis mine)*

Many people try to combine pastor and teacher here, believing that this should be one office. Often it is. But Paul's listing of the gifts in 1 Corinthians 12 is different, and distinguishes the gifts related to pastoring and teaching.

In many of our churches, however, we eliminate all of the gifts listed except for pastor. Evangelists are just pastors without a church sort of on a temporary assignment outside their field. Prophets are ignored. Apostles are either not mentioned, or are often given the title without being given the authority and the task of an apostle.

Don't go to the various lists of gifts and try to combine them all, and assume you have all the gifts. They are different because they are all just a sample of the work of the Holy Spirit. The key element throughout is to identify the working of the Holy Spirit.

Listening

In order to do so, we have to listen. If we listen, the Holy Spirit will tell us what our gifts are, and what gifts are available in our congregation, Sunday School class, or small group. If we listen, the Holy Spirit will tell us how to effectively use those gifts to perform the various functions and fill the various offices of the church.

The key to it all is listening!

Most of us were taught the use of a prism in science classes. You let white light pass through a prism, and it splits into various colors. Imagine the Holy Spirit as a reverse prism. Instead of splitting the light into various colors that separate and go their own way, he takes various colored beams and brings them together into a single source of light.

We are the various colored beams. If we will listen to the Holy Spirit, he will bring us together in just the right way to produce the single beam of God's light. That single beam can be called **effective ministry**.

The Holy Spirit is speaking . . . LISTEN!!!!

Now look at it from another perspective. We have seen that when people become unified and display the fruit of the Spirit, we can know that the Holy Spirit is active. Combining the fruit of the Spirit and the gifts in unity will build the body. Thus we can apply the building test to each action:

Will this build the body?

Church members frequently ask whether something they wish to do is good, whether it's scriptural, or whether Jesus would do it. These are all good questions, but they must be combined with another: Will this build the body? Why? Because a good action may nonetheless not be the **right or best** action in every time and place.

For example, Jesus cleansed the temple, driving out the money changers (Matthew 21:12-17, Mark 11:15-19, John 2:13-22). We assume that because Jesus did this, it was a good action. On another occasion he discussed the scripture with the elders in the temple (Luke 2:41-52). That was also a good action. But each of those actions had its time and its place.

At another time Jesus rebuked the Pharisees at considerable length, yet he was gentle with the woman taken in adultery. Both were good actions, but each had their time and place.

In order to be certain that a ministry or activity is appropriate in our church we need to make sure that it will build up the church at that time and in that place.

Is my focus on building the body?

This will determine whether our behavior in the church, in committees, study groups, or on work teams will build. If our focus is on the church and on glorifying Jesus Christ rather than on our own gratification or our own glory, then we will tend to behave in a way that tends to build.

> [1]*Christ encourages you, and his love comforts you. God's Spirit unites you, and you are concerned for others.* [2] *Now make me completely happy! Live in harmony by showing love for each other. Be united in what you think, as if you were only one person.* [3] *Don't be jealous or proud, but be humble and consider others more important than yourselves.* [4] *Care about them as much as you care about yourselves* [5] *and think the same way that Christ Jesus thought. – Philippians 2:1-5*

Is my motivation to build the body?

You are the only one who can answer this question. You can even focus on building the body for a wrong motivation. What's the problem, if it still builds? **You!** You will not be growing closer to Jesus and more filled with the Holy Spirit while you're looking for the glory for yourself. And if you find that you don't get the recognition, the money, or the respect that you think you are due, you might still get off track and start tearing the body down.

Gifts in Practice

Now let me give an illustration of how the various gifts might work in practice. This example is fictional, but I have seen every element of it happen in various services.

Suppose a visitor arrives at your church, and you know nothing about that person. Nobody invited him and nobody is introducing him to various church members. What should a Spirit led church do?

First, don't miss out on the things that good sense tells you to do. Observe and listen. You'll find some things out in ordinary ways. Often people who are used to listening for the Holy Spirit forget to listen to other human beings. They're so anxious to learn God's advanced strategies that they miss God's standard behavior. So don't forget the normal elements of hospitality.

But to go beyond that, what are some of the things that spiritual gifts can give you?

Perhaps there is a word of knowledge. Someone might simply realize that the visitor is a person in need of physical healing. That gives you something on which you can take action. Always remember God's standard behavior. Approach the person with love, courtesy, and respect.

I see very little difference between a prophetic word and a word of knowledge. In practice they seem to be different, but they work in a similar way. A prophetic word in this case could lead the worship leader to a particular song that might touch that person's heart. The prayer team might be led to pray about a particular stronghold during prayer time. The pastor might hear of a scripture that should be read or some particular message that should be given.

The message (or word) of wisdom might direct us to be careful, that this may be a person who has been hurt by church people before. How can we behave in a loving and non-hurtful manner? People who have the gift of words of wisdom are often neglected in the church, because the rest of us want to charge in and get things done, and we often would rather not be reminded of when caution is necessary. Some of us need the gift of listening to the ones God has gifted with wisdom!

The gift of healing is used in praying for the person at the appropriate time. One thing to accomplish in the sessions in which your group will discuss each individual's gift is to identify those who should be called on to pray for healing. Sometimes we're shy about acknowledging supernatural gifts because it seems like pride. Just remember that Balaam's donkey did God's work, so being an instrument should not be a source of pride.

At all times, intercessory prayer is appropriate, and can be guided by all of these same gifts. Instead of just praying generally, listen and then pray according to what you hear from the Holy Spirit.

Don't Get Stuck

Everything I have written here, and even what you will discuss in your group when you do the exercises is just a starting point. God will lead you outside of your normal paths and show you new ways to do ministry. As long as you are careful to listen to all of the guidance God has for you, you can proceed with confidence.

Questions and Exercises

1. Look at the number of times that build (or edify or another synonym) occurs in 1 Corinthians 14. Does this tell us something about the importance of building?

____

____

2. Concordance Exercise: Look up "edify," "build," or whatever word your Bible translation uses in 1 Corinthians 14 and examine some other passages that use this word. What are some characteristics of building in the Bible?

____

____

____

____

____

3. Look up each of the major offices of the church listed in Ephesians 4 in your Bible Dictionary. Can you get a clear picture of what each one does?

____

____

____

4. Read 1 Corinthinas 12-14. Describe what you think a Corinthian church service was like.

____

____

____

____

____

____

Identifying Your Gifts

Most programs dealing with spiritual gifts in the church take a largely psychological approach. The key element is a survey, on which you discover where your talents are. You can learn something about spiritual gifts in that way. But I believe that the key to truly identifying spiritual gifts is by listening to the Holy Spirit.

Listening to the Holy Spirit can discover:

- ✔ Gifts that you didn't know you had
- ✔ Gifts that make you uncomfortable, so you might ignore them
- ✔ Gifts that the church needs, but that you may not have recognized
- ✔ Gifts that are being underutilized
- ✔ Gifts you think you have when actually you don't

Listening is very important in scripture.

> ***Listen**, Israel! . . . – Deuteronomy 6:4*
>
> *My friends, I beg you to **listen** as I teach. – Psalm 78:1*
>
> *If you have ears, **pay attention**. – Mark 4:9*

If you have ears, ***listen*** *to what the Spirit says to the churches. – Revelation 2:7 (emphasis mine)*

We are frequently concerned with whether God is listening to our prayers. But did you know that God was testing to see whether we are listening to him?

12 *Your luck will end!*
I will see to it that you
are slaughtered with swords.
You ***refused to answer***
when I called out;
you ***paid no attention***
to my instructions.
Instead, you did what I hated,
knowing it was wrong. – Isaiah 65:12 (emphasis mine)

All of these texts emphasize the fact that God wants us to pay attention to what he has to say. Because of these many instances when God tells us to listen, I've based this program from identifying your gifts on listening—both to the Holy Spirit, and to one another.

Some people want to hear from God, but are not anxious to hear from other church members. They just want to hear from God directly. But God will often give you a message only through someone else in the body. That keeps the body healthy by making us work together and work out our problems.

But if we say we love God and don't love each other, we are liars. We cannot see God. So how can we love God, if we don't love the people we can see? – 1 John 4:20

God connects our love for him with our love for one another. That's one of the reasons the gifts are given to different people in the body—

so we can learn to work together, use our gifts, and build both our own character and that of the church congregation.

Did you know that a congregation has a character? We are much too willing to separate ourselves from our congregation. “I'm alright, but my congregation is spiritually dead.” Be very careful when you say something like that, because you are like a cell in a dead body. Unless the whole is brought to life, you will accomplish very little.

Let's look at 1 John 4:20 as a hearing-loving analogy:

> If someone says, “I listen to God,” but he doesn't listen to his brother, he's a liar. For how can one who doesn't listen to his brother, whom he has seen, listen to God, whom he has not seen.

We must listen to one another.

Paul expressed this in a different way:

> *3 Don't be jealous or proud, but be humble and consider others more important than yourselves. 4 Care about them as much as you care about yourselves 5 and think the same way that Christ Jesus thought. – Philippians 2:3-5*

We have mutual need, and it can be fulfilled as part of the body of Christ:

- ✔ You have a need to serve
- ✔ You have a need to be served
- ✔ We have a need to serve one another

Step #1: Listening

Purpose: To hear what other members of the body have seen in each person, and what each hears from the Holy Spirit about the gifts of others

Background: "Spirit Led Ministry" and "Identifying Your Gifts" audio from the Pacesetters Bible School News Blog (biblepacesetter.org/news, category *Spiritual Gifts*) by Henry Neufeld, and chapters *The Holy Spirit and Spiritual Gifts, Identifiying Your Gifts,* and *Spirit Led Ministry.*

Time: Up to 2 minutes per person, but normally less; 12-20 minutes total

Activity:

1. Offer a prayer, focusing on listening, surrender to the Holy Spirit, and honesty

2. Go around the group person by person and . . .

   - ✔ Have the group members identify each person's gifts, other than their own. It is valid to speak from observation or from what one believes the Holy Spirit has revealed.
   - ✔ Each person should be brief and specific
   - ✔ Give examples only if asked
   - ✔ Do your best not to embarrass anyone, do your best not to be embarrassed
   - ✔ If someone is identifying your gift, LISTEN.
   - ✔ Take time to listen to the Holy Spirit
   - ✔ Take notes in the space provided

3. Ask each person to summarize what they have heard

4. Pray again to seal the activity

> Listening is just that: LISTENING! It doesn't imply agreement. It doesn't require agreement.

Step #2: Expressing

Purpose: To express what each member of the group understands about his or her gifts; to learn to express publicly what God has done for and through you.

Time: Up to 2 minutes per person, but normally less; 12-20 minutes total

Activity:

1. Offer a prayer, emphasizing grace, surrender to the Spirit, self-examination and listening to the Holy Spirit
2. Share, emphasizing the following
   - ✔ Identify your own gifts
   - ✔ Listen to the Holy Spirit
   - ✔ What gifts do you know you have?
   - ✔ Do you understand what others have said about your gifts?
3. Discuss any differences in what was revealed in the two sessions. Do not be judgmental or try to force one understanding on everyone in the group. Just examine, question, and seek understanding.
4. Seal what you just did with prayer.

Step #3: Examining

Once you have listened to others talk about your gifts and in turn talked about your own, it's time to refine what you have learned. To help you do this, I have prepared a survey. At least it's sort of a survey. It looks like a survey, you fill it out like a survey, you calculate your results like you would if it were a survey, but you need to think about it differently.

In designing a survey, the precise choice of wording in the questions is important. The designer wants to make sure that the readers understand the question and that responses will be consistent so that the survey will produce valid data.

I designed this survey in a substantially different way. These questions are not designed to get you to tell what you already know; they are designed to get you thinking and possibly to challenge some of your assumptions about yourself. When you talked about your gifts, you probably based most of what you said on your experience. I hope you learned to hear from the Holy Spirit as well, but most of what you said probably came from what seems comfortable to you. That's not a bad thing. In fact, it's almost impossible to avoid.

The survey, on the other hand, will give you some ideas of ministries that you may not have considered. That's important. You need to try to get beyond any limitations you have placed on yourself. So as you answer the survey, be as honest as possible, but let the questions stimulate your thinking.

In the times that I have given this survey, the results have actually been more accurate than I intended, but they are still less accurate than a questionnaire that was designed as a scientific survey. What is most important is that you think about each result, and compare it with what others in the group have told you they see as your gifts. Don't simply reject a result because it makes you uncomfortable In many cases, people reevaluate their gifts, and other members of the group will help them with focus.

Again, in an ordinary survey, I would generally ask you to respond to a question quickly, giving your first impression. On this survey, take a bit of time to think. The idea here is to ask yourself whether you really enjoy a particular activity and whether you have considered that activity at all.

The Gifts Survey

Plan a complete session to complete, evaluate, and discuss the survey. Since this survey is not just about getting a set of numbers, but more about getting you thinking, you will want the time to think and discuss. Keep in mind the things you have already learned as you discussed your gifts with one another.

Don't decide to take the survey results over what you learned in that discussion. Evaluate **both**, listen to what others tell you, and then **pray and listen to the Holy Spirit**. The Holy Spirit gives the gifts as he wishes, and he is the final voice you should hear on the subject.

Services Questionnaire

Instructions

For each statement mark a number from 1 to 5 indicating how fulfilling you would find that activity, with '1' indicating that you do not like that activity at all or disagree strongly with the statement and '5' indicating that you would choose it above all others, or agree strongly. Be honest. Do not answer as you think you ought to, but rather as you actually feel.

Questionnaire

	Disagree				Agree
1. I like to work with underprivileged children.	1	2	3	4	5
2. Others in church often ask me to pray for them.	1	2	3	4	5
3. I am often led to pray for other people.	1	2	3	4	5
4. I feel a great burden for those who do not know Jesus.	1	2	3	4	5
5. I like to meet new people and talk to them about things that are important to me.	1	2	3	4	5
6. I would rather prepare a meal in the fellowship hall than join in a small prayer group.	1	2	3	4	5
7. I like to discuss the Bible with others in a small group.	1	2	3	4	5
8. I often feel that the Lord is speaking to me.	1	2	3	4	5
9. If I have a choice, I'd prefer to teach a children's Sunday School class.	1	2	3	4	5
10. You need to take care of people's physical needs before you worry about their spiritual needs.	1	2	3	4	5

	Disagree				Agree
11. It's OK to feed people, but if we don't reach them for Christ, we're wasting our time.	1	2	3	4	5
12. I am comfortable in front of large groups.	1	2	3	4	5
13. Others listen when I speak.	1	2	3	4	5
14. When someone comes into church who is ill, I long to pray for their healing.	1	2	3	4	5
15. I like to visit hospitals and cheer people up.	1	2	3	4	5
16. People like to have me visit because they tell me I'm an encouragement to them.	1	2	3	4	5
17. Others tell me that I help them understand the scriptures.	1	2	3	4	5
18. I would like to see more pictures and banners in church.	1	2	3	4	5
19. I don't mind knocking on people's doors to invite them to a church event.	1	2	3	4	5
20. It's easy for me to start a conversation about my faith.	1	2	3	4	5
21. Children tend to gather around me because they know I love them.	1	2	3	4	5
22. Young people say that they like to listen to what I have to say.	1	2	3	4	5

	Disagree				Agree
23. Young people say that I'm a good listener.	1	2	3	4	5
24. I like to deliver food to the needy.	1	2	3	4	5
25. I want the church to look good inside and out!	1	2	3	4	5
26. I'd be willing to cancel a meeting if we could manage to keep the church a little bit cleaner and more presentable.	1	2	3	4	5
27. I love to read scripture.	1	2	3	4	5
28. Tithing is important and should be regularly emphasized in our worship services.	1	2	3	4	5
29. I am gratified to see money that I have given used in God's work.	1	2	3	4	5
30. I am anxious to see the gospel spread throughout the world.	1	2	3	4	5
31. I find it easy to get along with people of other cultures.	1	2	3	4	5
32. My favorite part of worship is singing and praising the Lord.	1	2	3	4	5
33. When I'm joyful I just have to dance!	1	2	3	4	5
34. I firmly believe that God can and will heal people today.	1	2	3	4	5

	Disagree				Agree
35. Sometimes I find that the only way I can express myself to God is by speaking in tongues.	1	2	3	4	5
36. We need to hear regular solid teaching of the Word of God.	1	2	3	4	5
37. I like to collect the offering.	1	2	3	4	5
38. I like to urge people to give to the Lord.	1	2	3	4	5
39. When I hear the mission of the church proclaimed, I can practically see it fulfilled!	1	2	3	4	5
40. The most important thing we can do is get people to decide for Jesus.	1	2	3	4	5
41. If we don't teach people to follow Jesus every day, we could be wasting our efforts in getting decisions for Christ.	1	2	3	4	5
42. I'd like to see banners waved or carried in procession on a regular basis.	1	2	3	4	5
43. I like to sing in the praise choir.	1	2	3	4	5
44. I'd rather get with a small group and pray, even through church service sometimes.	1	2	3	4	5
45. Sometimes I just find myself speaking in tongues.	1	2	3	4	5

	Disagree				Agree
46. We need to get outside the walls of our church and reach the community.	1	2	3	4	5
47. We need to have an active program in foreign missions.	1	2	3	4	5
48. We need more training so that we will know how to carry out the church's mission.	1	2	3	4	5
49. I prefer to just soak in the presence of God.	1	2	3	4	5
50. Once I catch the vision, I have the faith to believe God will help us carry it out.	1	2	3	4	5

Survey Results Sheet

Instructions: (Please follow these instructions exactly. This chart can be complicated.) For each question, listed from 1 to 50 at the left, enter the number you circled in every white square in the 16 columns to the right. You will be entering one number multiple times in many rows. Total all the numbers in each column, and put the result in the "ST" (subtotal) row at the bottom of the page.

Just follow the steps. Do not try to understand—yet!

	1	2	3	4	5	6	7	8	9	10	11	12	13	14	15	16
1																
2																
3																
4																
5																
6																
7																
8																
9																
10																
11																
12																
13																
14																
15																
16																
17																
18																
19																
20																
21																
22																
23																
24																
25																
ST																

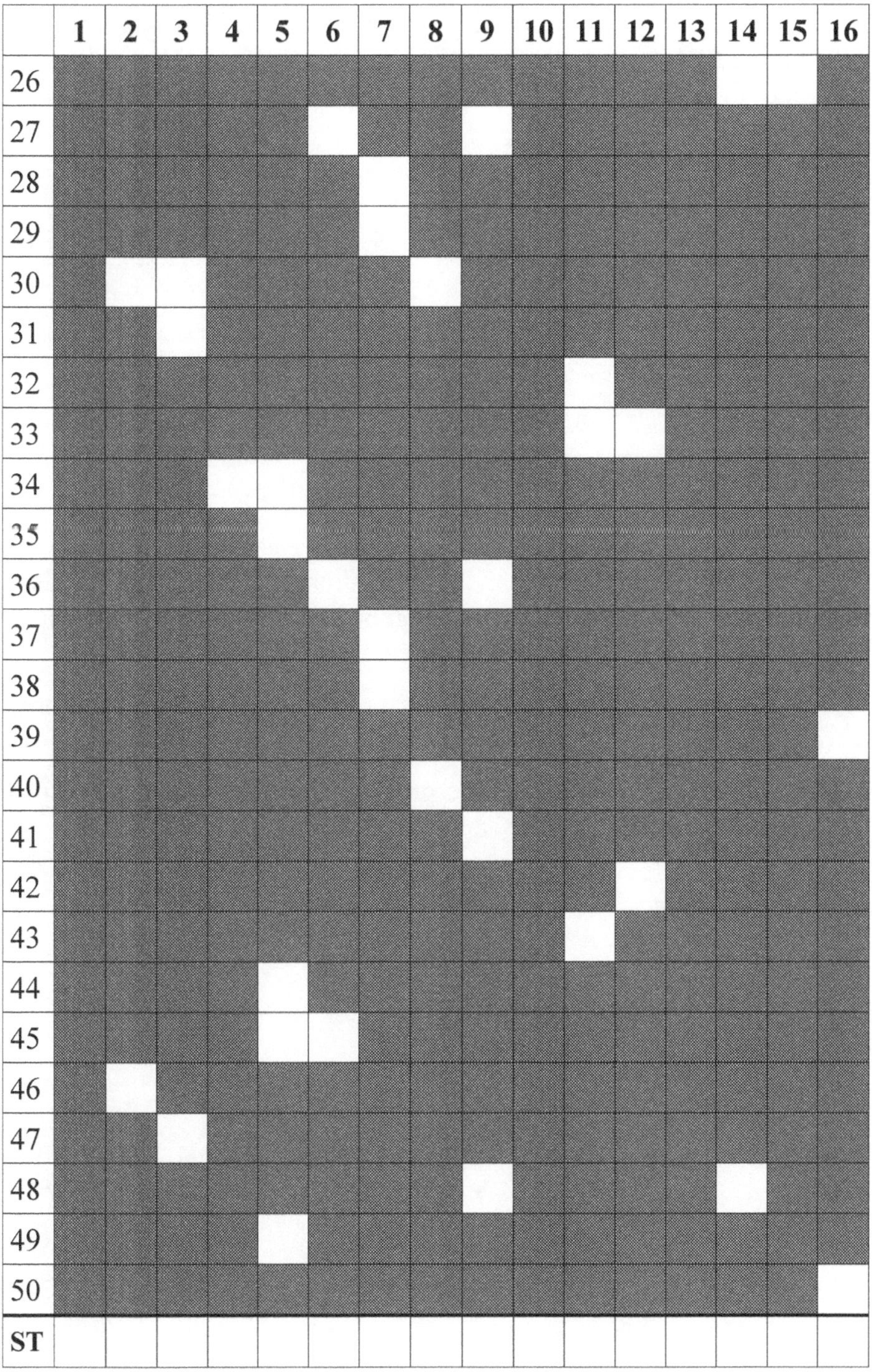
1 2 3 4 5 6 7 8 9 10 11 12 13 14 15 16
26
27
28
29
30
31
32
33
34
35
36
37
38
39
40
41
42
43
44
45
46
47
48
49
50
ST

Now copy the subtotals for each column from the first page into the row marked **P1**, and those from the second page into the row marked **P2**, and then total them, placing the numbers in the bottom row, marked **T**.

	1	**2**	**3**	**4**	**5**	**6**	**7**	**8**	**9**	**10**	**11**	**12**	**13**	**14**	**15**	**16**
P1																
P2																
T																

Interpreting Your Results

Instructions:

- ✔ Enter the Number for the total column in the matching ministry box. The ministry box is numbered according to the sixteen columns (1=Children, 2=Outreach, and so forth).
- ✔ Using a calculator, divide the number by the "Max" number, multiply by 100, and enter your result in the score column.
- ✔ The higher your score, the greater your interest and gifting for that particular ministry area.

#	Ministry	Result	/ Max	Score	Note
X	***Example***	***8***	***/ 15***	***53%***	***8 / 15 x 100 = 53%***
1	Children		/ 15	%	
2	Outreach		/ 45	%	
3	Missions		/ 30	%	
4	Prayer Ministry		/ 30	%	
5	Intercession		/ 40	%	
6	Proclamation		/ 50	%	
7	Stewardship		/ 20	%	
8	Evangelism		/ 35	%	
9	Teaching		/ 40	%	
10	Youth		/ 10	%	
11	Music		/ 20	%	
12	Visual Arts		/ 15	%	
13	Hospitality		/ 15	%	
14	Administration		/ 10	%	
15	Helping		/ 30	%	
16	Leadership		/ 15	%	

Note: Keep in mind that this is not a scientific survey. That is intentional. This is a tool to stimulate your thinking and your conversation with other members of your church family in order to discover where you belong in ministry. Some questions were chosen especially to get discussion going. Don't decide that because your score reads a certain thing, that is what you must do in ministry. It should only be a tool used to help you hear God's direction and drop your own agendas.

The best way to evaluate this survey is using a computer. On the Energion Publications web site there is a form you can use to evaluate the survey results. There is also a spreadsheet available for download on the Energion Publications web site To find these items, go to our web site page for this product (http://www.energionpubs.com/ep_detail.php?sku=1893729478) and follow the links.

Learning from the Questionnaire

Did the questions help you identify any areas of service that you may have neglected to consider as a way to serve God and his children?

Are there areas of service you may be trying to accomplish for which you are not equipped?

Finding Your Place in the Body

The last two steps in this program ask you to look not only at yourself, but at the whole church body of which you are a part. What are the needs of the church as a whole? Are you fulfilling the role to which God has called you in that particular situation?

You will need to continue to build your listening skills. The entire group should concentrate on listening to each person as they speak. As always, the best answer is not necessarily the one that makes you most comfortable, but rather one that is most likely to build your congregation and your community.

In Step #5 you will need your pastor or a designated church leader to attend. This must be a person who can either help people find a place for ministry or can set up appointments to see the pastor or a church leader and discuss their part in the ministry of the church.

Remember: This entire process is a failure if you don't end up serving where God has called you to serve!

Step #4: Fitting

Materials: Results of the first three steps

Purpose: Prayerfully discuss what you have learned and clarify what is God's call on your life and in your church

Time: 2 minutes per person, 12-20 minutes.

You have listened to others discuss your gifts. You have expressed the gifts you believe you have received from God. You have used a survey to examine where you may be called to serve in your church congregation and in your community.

The question remains: *What is **God** calling me to do?*

Not everything that others see as your gifts and calling will be what God has called you to do. You may have missed some things. This is a chance to prayerfully discuss things that may have troubled you about the results of the survey, or comments that people in the group have made about you, or even comments you have heard from time to time from people elsewhere.

This is a time of **focus**.

Activity:

Prayer – set aside agendas and resentments, open ears to hear what God is saying, be willing to express and listen, and surrender to the one Spirit.

In turn have each member of the group discuss any questions that have been raised by the preceding discussion and survey.

Are there gifts others have identified in you that you do not believe you have? Why do they believe you have that gift?

Do you believe you have gifts others have not identified? Discuss these with the group.

Do your gifts and services support one another? Am I working in areas now that I am gifted in?

Have you identified new gifts through any of these activities? Do you know how you are to use them?

Have you identified gifts which are not used in any of the areas of ministry in which you are involved?

Have you learned about any new areas of service that you should consider?

Have you heard God's call to something specific during this time?

Seal what you have done with prayer.

Disagreement about gifts and how to use them is **not** disunity unless you fight over it.

Step #5: Unifying

People: Invite the church pastor or a designated member of the church's leadership to participate

Materials: Your church's mission statement or similar document

Purpose: Examine what you know about your gifts and the areas in which God has called you to work in the light of your congregation's mission

Time: 2 minutes per person, 12-20 minutes.

Activity:

1. Prayer, focusing on unity of the body and our ability to serve our church and community with our gifts
2. Read the mission statement of the church
3. In turn have each person state
    a. Where they are serving and how that helps to accomplish the mission of the church
4. Where they think they should be serving, tying in their call and gifts to the mission of the church
5. Seek input from the pastoral representative at each stage
6. ***Note:*** *This is not a time for appointment to offices, and changes in the church's procedures. There are appropriate times and places for that. This is a time to ask how you individually fit into the corporate calling of the body. Don't get off track. Don't start, encourage, or allow a complaint session.*

Follow-up: Meet with your pastor or a designated leader to discuss your gifts and your place in the ministry of your church

Note to Pastor: Be prepared to have an open time in your schedule to place appointments.

Pastor/Leader	Date	Time

Getting Focused on Your Mission

Identify ways in which you can bring your gifts and your service more into line with your church's specific mission.

Are there any new areas in which you intend to get involved? List them.

Did you find some areas you thought you were called to, but that didn't fit in with the mission?

Notes:

Mentoring Others

[18] Jesus came to them and said:

I have been given all authority in heaven and on earth! [19] Go to the people of all nations and make them my disciples. Baptize them in the name of the Father, the Son, and the Holy Spirit, [20] and teach them to do everything I have told you. I will be with you always, even until the end of the world.– Matthew 28:18-20

When Jesus gave the gospel commission, he seems to ask all of us to be teachers. At least he wants us to make disciples, which involves teaching—"teach them to do everything I have told you." This is not a command for the few, the special, the extraordinary, or just those who are ordained. It's a command for all of us.

But many of us find easy to follow. Some people become fearful when someone talks about teaching, mentoring, or discipling others. Perhaps they remember James 3:1, "My friends, we should not all try to become teachers. In fact, teachers will be judged more strictly than others."

But while not all church members will hold the office of teacher, preach, or even teach a Sunday School class, the vast majority will have an influence on the lives of other people in the church. When the hospitality team provides a friendly greeting to visitors and members, new Christians will be watching. When any member prays for another, there will be other people watching. When any leader sends someone else to do a task, he or she takes on a certain amount of a mentoring role.

Merriam-Webster's Collegiate Dictionary (10th edition) defines a mentor as "a trusted counselor or guide." A mentor may teach by talking, but more often, a mentor teaches by doing and by allowing others to do, then empowering them to do it on their own.

A key part of becoming an effective church leader involves the following:

- **Discipling others**
  Discipling is a large subject in itself, but it can be summarized by Paul's words, "You must follow my example, as I follow the example of Christ" (1 Corinthians 11:1).

- **Equipping others for ministry**
  This involves both discipling/mentoring and the more traditional role of teacher, giving people the training they need to acomplish the task, and making them aware of their gifts.

- **Empowering people to do ministry**
  When we empower, we let church members know that they have the authority and the ability to accomplish a mission, and that they have the permission of the leadership to go ahead and do so. Don't assume a church member knows just because *you* know. Tell them. Make it clear.

- **Releasing others to do ministry**
  Many would include releasing under empowering, but I separate it. Many times leaders will *observe* that someone has the gifts and the training, tell them it is OK to work, and then step in and interfere with what they do. You may be able to do the job better, but you

will never be able to relinquish that job and get on with God's next call if you don't release.

In order to accomplish these goals, let's look at the difference between the world's pattern of teaching and the Christian goal.

The world's pattern of teaching says: "I'm the expert. Shut up and listen! Make me look good when this training is over."

Many of you will believe I'm being unfair here. You have seen many teachers outside of the church's setting who are dedicated, unselfish, and are not arrogant. Many of you will have encountered teachers in the church who fit my "world" pattern quite well.

That doesn't surprise me. We shouldn't assume that just because people aren't in church, they can't do good things. Many things that happen in the world outside the church are good. We could benefit by learning from them. There are management techniques as well as teaching and mentoring methods that could be beneficial to the church. What will distinguish us from the world is not that we do everything differently, but rather that we filter everything we do through the example and law of Jesus Christ.

So I do not distinguish the world's way from the *church's* way; I distinguish the world's way from *Christ's* way. Christ's way can be followed in church or outside. It's tragic, however, when Christ's church doesn't use his way of teaching.

Seven Principles from Jesus

Let's extract Christ's way from an example of his teaching in John 4. I like this passage particularly because it shows Jesus starting with a student who has no interest, and finishes with that student going out to make more disciples. It gives us the whole pattern in one place.

We start with John 4:3 –

[3] Jesus left Judea and started for Galilee again. [4] This time he had to go through Samaria, [5] and on his way he came to the town of Sychar. It was near the field that Jacob had long ago given to his son Joseph. [6-8] The well that Jacob had dug was still there, and Jesus sat down beside it because he was tired from traveling. It was noon, and after Jesus' disciples had gone into town to buy some food, a Samaritan woman came to draw water from the well. – John 4:3-8

Notice first that Jesus observes. He doesn't go out to meet the woman. He sees what she is doing and who she is.

- ✔ The first principle of Christian mentoring is observing and listening. You must know the need of the person you wish to teach and know what will get their attention. Listen both to the Holy Spirit and to the person.

Jesus asked her, "Would you please give me a drink of water?"

[9] "You are a Jew," she replied, "and I am a Samaritan woman. How can you ask me for a drink of water when Jews and Samaritans won't have anything to do with each other?" – John 4:8b-9

Jesus involves and even shocks his listener. Imagine her surprise when she finds that this Jewish man actually sees her. He doesn't ignore her. He makes a request. Often we want to serve others because we know we are supposed to serve others. But are you willing also to allow others to serve you?

One weekend I was part of a prayer team for a seminar on prayer. Throughout the seminar I had been watching and trying to encourage one gentleman who I knew was called to prayer ministry, but he wouldn't step out and get involved. Nothing I said seemed to do any good.

On the last night of the seminar I invited him to the altar, expressed a genuine need of my own, and asked him to pray for me. He was surprised, but did as I asked. That seemed to liberate him from the idea that "official" prayer team members who had come from another church were the only ones capable of praying. For the rest of the evening he engaged in ministry to others, and of course received ministry himself. Sometimes you have to provide someone with an opportunity to experience the blessing of service.

- ✔ The second principle of Christ's teaching method is to engage the person at their point of interest.

> *10 Jesus answered, "You don't know what God wants to give you, and you don't know who is asking you for a drink. If you did, you would ask me for the water that gives life."*
>
> *11 "Sir," the woman said, "you don't even have a bucket, and the well is deep. Where are you going to get this life-giving water? 12 Our ancestor Jacob dug this well for us, and his family and animals got water from it. Are you greater than Jacob?"*
>
> *13 Jesus answered, "Everyone who drinks this water will get thirsty again. 14 But no one who drinks the water I give will ever be thirsty again. The water I give is like a flowing fountain that gives eternal life."*
>
> *15 The woman replied, "Sir, please give me a drink of that water! Then I won't get thirsty and have to come to this well again." – John 4:10-15*

Jesus takes the response to his simple question and starts to expand it. He begins with something that clearly interests the woman, the need for water, and draws her from that into her concern with social niceties and with relations between peoples.

At the same time he doesn't lose his focus. His plan all the time is to give her living water. He responds to who she is and what she is interested in, but he knows what she needs.

Notice that Jesus doesn't require complete understanding as he moves along. He will introduce more and more of what he knows this woman needs as he goes along, but in verse 15 we can clearly see that the woman doesn't really understand what Jesus is talking about. She's still concerned about well water. In order to break past this, Jesus needs to apply some more of God's power—subtly in this case, without lightning bolts!

- ✔ The third principle is to expand their point of interest to lead to thinking about their need.

> 16 *Jesus told her, "Go and bring your husband."*
>
> 17-18 *The woman answered, "I don't have a husband."*
>
> *"That's right," Jesus replied, "you're telling the truth. You don't have a husband. You have already been married five times, and the man you are now living with isn't your husband." – John 4:16-18*

This is a use of spiritual gifts. Do you disagree? Do you say, "This is Jesus! This is something special?" It *is* special, but it is also *available*. Words of knowledge or the gift of prophecy would certainly cover this situation. Something needs to get this woman beyond the need to get physical water from the well in front of her. Supernatural knowledge is what will accomplish that.

The spiritual gifts needed may be different, but don't neglect spiritual gifts at any point in teaching or in approaching new people with the gospel message. I see two common errors. Some people who believe in the gifts of the Spirit start depending solely on the Holy Spirit speaking to them. But the same God who sent the Holy Spirit gave you eyes, ears, and a brain. Jesus didn't need supernatural power to comprehend the basics. The woman is coming to the well alone, not at the proper time. She's Samaritan. He knows there is some kind of rejection going on here, and he knows that she will be shocked by his question.

But in order to get her off her topic, and onto the more important target, he needs something more. So he applies the spiritual gifts.

- ✔ The fourth principle is to apply spiritual gifts. This may occur at any point, though it is fourth in our example.

> *19 The woman said, "Sir, I can see that you are a prophet.*
> *20 My ancestors worshiped on this mountain, [r]but you*
> *Jews say Jerusalem is the only place to worship."*
>
> *21 Jesus said to her:*
>
> *Believe me, the time is coming when you won't worship the*
> *Father either on this mountain or in Jerusalem. 22 You*
> *Samaritans don't really know the one you worship. But we*
> *Jews do know the God we worship, and by using us, God*
> *will save the world. 23 But a time is coming, and it is*
> *already here! Even now the true worshipers are being led*
> *by the Spirit to worship the Father according to the truth.*
> *These are the ones the Father is seeking to worship him. 24*
> *God is Spirit, and those who worship God must be led by*
> *the Spirit to worship him according to the truth.*

[25] The woman said, "I know that the Messiah will come. He is the one we call Christ. When he comes, he will explain everything to us."[26] "I am that one," Jesus told her, "and I am speaking to you now." – John 4:19-26

- ✔ The fifth principle is to come home at the right point with the message.

Jesus is the answer to this woman's real needs—not her need for water from the well which is, as she pointed out, easily fulfilled if one has a bucket, but her need for spiritual healing.

[27] The disciples returned about this time and were surprised to find Jesus talking with a woman. But none of them asked him what he wanted or why he was talking with her. – John 4:27

- ✔ The sixth principle is that some, even in the church, will not understand what you're doing. Don't be distracted from your mission by the misunderstanding of your allies.

[28] The woman left her water jar and ran back into town. She said to the people, [29] "Come and see a man who told me everything I have ever done! Could he be the Messiah?" [30] Everyone in town went out to see Jesus. – John 4:28-29

- ✔ The seventh principle is to produce and use testimony.

When we make disciples, we are not just trying to put notches on our belt of put new meat on the church's reports. We're creating disciples, and disciples are people with a testimony.

Again, you may find it difficult to see this woman as a disciple, but as soon as she gets excited about the message and starts going and calling others, she has started on the path of discipleship. Don't make the mistake of equating discipleship with perfection or completion.

Learning from the Sanctuary Service

While we look to Jesus as the ultimate example of a teacher, there are many other examples of good teaching in the Bible. In the books of the Pentateuch we find the laws that defined the temple ritual and much of the life of the Israelites. When Paul called the law "our teacher" (Galatians 3:24) he meant more than that the law teaches us that our own works cannot bring us to salvation. The law was, in fact, designed to teach the people skills needed for holy living.

As an example, consider Leviticus 6:1-7, which describes an offering for a trespass. But there is an important difference in this ritual. Unlike the ones immediately before and after it, it does not talk about inadvertent sins, but rather about actions that would require intention. At the same time it provides a teaching in the form of a ritual about repentance.

> *1 The LORD spoke to Moses, saying: 2 When any of you sin and commit a trespass against the LORD by deceiving a neighbor in a matter of a deposit or a pledge, or by robbery, or if you have defrauded a neighbor, 3 or have found something lost and lied about it—if you swear falsely regarding any of the various things that one may do and sin thereby— . . . – Leviticus 6:1-3 (NRSV)*

Notice the list of sins here. If you have lied to your neighbor or defrauded him, or lied about finding a lost object, or even sworn falsely, this is your sacrifice. Why is a separate sacrifice ritual required? Because almost all of the sacrifices applied only to sins that were committed inadvertently. Repentance is the key to forgiveness and atonement.

[4] when you have sinned and realize your guilt, and would restore what you took by robbery or by fraud or the deposit that was committed to you, or the lost thing that you found, [5] or anything else about which you have sworn falsely, . . . – Leviticus 6:4-5a (NRSV)

The sacrifice is brought when you realize your guilt. Very rarely do we see the full nature of our sin when we are committing it. We may know, but we don't really realize. We don't allow it to come to our full awareness. As the Holy Spirit works on our mind, we will become aware of our guilt and realize the need for reconciliation with God.

. . . you shall repay the principal amount and shall add one-fifth to it. You shall pay it to its owner when you realize your guilt. . . . – Leviticus 6:5b (NRSV)

True repentance starts with a desire to make things right as much as possible. There are often things that only God can heal that result from our wrongdoing, but to whatever extent we can, we are called to make restitution.

[6] And you shall bring to the priest, as your guilt offering to the LORD, a ram without blemish from the flock, or its equivalent, for a guilt offering. – Leviticus 6:6 (NRSV)

The sacrifice is brought, reminding us of sin, of its cost, and providing a public testimony of repentance. For Christians the key element here is the public confession. When we repent we claim the sacrifice of Jesus, but we need to make our testimony public.

[7] The priest shall make atonement on your behalf before the LORD, and you shall be forgiven for any of the things that one may do and incur guilt thereby. – Leviticus 6:7 (NRSV)

The priest performs the ritual and provides the public form, but God does the forgiving.

Some principles of teaching and mentoring taught in this passage are:

- ✔ Repetition – each time a person sinned, he had to repeat a set of actions.
- ✔ Visual – the actions could be seen and identified, and the ritual illustrated what was happening spiritually.
- ✔ Action – the person doesn't merely talk or make a mental assent. He carries out a set of actions.
- ✔ Involvement – the humans get involved in the action. It's not just the priest that speaks and acts, while the repentant sinner stands idly by. Both become involved, knowing all the time that God is the one who will forgive.

Learning from History

Much of the teaching in the Bible comes through historical events. As Christians we believe that God has acted in the world. These actions have been designed to bring each of us to salvation. We can learn by reading and thinking about this history.

The books of Joshua, Judges, Samuel, Kings, and Chronicles are major examples of this type of teaching. In this teaching you will find again that repetition is a key element. In Kings we don't have just one king who is bad, we have many. We have many stories of revival and reformation, and again many stories of backsliding.

Testimony

In discussing the way Jesus taught we concluded with seeing how a testimony was produced that could, in turn, bring others to Jesus. Each of us has at least one thing we can use in teaching others—our testimony. No matter how little you know about anything else, you do know what God has done in your own life. Practice sharing your testimony with others.

A testimony need not be limited to your salvation story. Each thing that you have accomplished in your walk with Jesus becomes part of your testimony. Perhaps it was the first time you read scripture in a study group, or participated in Sunday School. There's someone in your congregation who hasn't done those things yet. Perhaps it was the first time you participated in the worship service. Again, there are folks out there who haven't done that.

By sharing your testimony—the simple story of how God helped you do each new thing—you help others to learn how to do the same thing. You may think your testimony is small and unimportant, but it may be the one thing that someone else needs to help them get started.

Intergenerational testimonies are particularly critical. Notice how the psalmist highlights the "telling" through four generations. I've provided numbers to the side and printed the generational "tellings" in bold print.

> 1 *Give ear, O my people, to my teaching;*
> *incline your ears to the words of my mouth.*
> 2 *I will open my mouth in a parable;*
> *I will utter dark sayings from of old,*
> 3 *things that we have heard and known,*
> *that our* ***ancestors*** *have told us.*
> 4 *We will not hide them from* ***their children****;*
> *we will tell to the* ***coming generation***
> *the glorious deeds of the* L*ORD*, *and his might,*
> *and the wonders that he has done.*
>
> 5 *He established a decree in Jacob,*
> *and appointed a law in Israel,*
> *which he commanded our* ***ancestors*** (1)

to teach to ***their children****;* 2
6 *that the* ***next generation*** *might know them,*
the ***children yet unborn****,* 3
and rise up and tell them to ***their children****,* 4
7 *so that they should set their hope in God,*
and not forget the works of God,
but keep his commandments;
8 *and that they should not be like their ancestors,*
a stubborn and rebellious generation,
a generation whose heart was not steadfast,
whose spirit was not faithful to God.
– Psalm 78:1-8 (NRSV)

I believe this Psalm is a charter for Christian education. The primary focus of Christian education is to pass on our testimony to the next generation. That is what each person is called to do. Some of us are called to do it in a more academic manner. All are called to do it to someone at some time.

Following Jesus in Teaching

Earlier, we learned from what Jesus did as he encountered the woman at the well, drew her into conversation and concluded with her sharing her own testimony of Jesus. Now let's look again at Jesus in action, this time at how Jesus himself worked, then made disciples, and empowered them for ministry.

Experience

Experience produces testimony. Some would prefer to say that testing produces testimony, but it is experience that tests us. Jesus himself began his ministry with experience, and he set out on his task with a testimony.

> *9 About that time Jesus came from Nazareth in Galilee,*
> *and John baptized him in the Jordan River. 10 As soon as*
> *Jesus came out of the water, he saw the sky open and the*
> *Holy Spirit coming down to him like a dove. 11 A voice*
> *from heaven said, "You are my own dear Son, and I am*
> *pleased with you."*
>
> *12 Right away God's Spirit made Jesus go into the desert.*
> *13 He stayed there for forty days while Satan tested him.*
> *Jesus was with the wild animals, but angels took care of*
> *him. – Mark 1:9-13*

Jesus receives two experiences here: Empowerment and testing. Sometimes we think of Jesus as never having to learn, but if that were the case, how could he possibly be "tempted in every way that we are?" Indeed, Luke tells us explicitly that Jesus grew and **increased** in both wisdom and stature (Luke 2:52).

Demonstration

Following that experience, Jesus went out to demonstrate. He put into practice the things that he would tell his disciples to do.

> *21 Jesus and his disciples went to the town of Capernaum.*
> *Then on the next Sabbath he went into the Jewish meeting*
> *place and started teaching. 22 Everyone was amazed at his*
> *teaching. He taught with authority, and not like the*
> *teachers of the Law of Moses. 23 Suddenly a man with an*
> *evil spirit in him entered the meeting place and yelled, 24*
> *"Jesus from Nazareth, what do you want with us? Have*
> *you come to destroy us? I know who you are! You are*
> *God's Holy One."*

25 Jesus told the evil spirit, "Be quiet and come out of the
man!" 26 The spirit shook him. Then it gave a loud shout
and left.

27 Everyone was completely surprised and kept saying to
each other, "What is this? It must be some new kind of
powerful teaching! Even the evil spirits obey him." 28
News about Jesus quickly spread all over Galilee. – Mark
1:21-28

Jesus teaches, demonstrating the way in which he had been empowered by the Spirit, and utilizing the authority he received by being tested during his temptation. His disciples saw Jesus in action and thus knew what was possible.

Frequently we use our imperfection as an excuse for not carrying out ministry and demonstrating the power of God. "Do as I say, not as I do" is a cliché, because it responds to a human weakness. We know that we make mistakes, and we don't want others to follow those mistakes. But as Christian leaders who claim that Jesus can transform our lives we have to live and demonstrate that transformation through personal pursuit of holiness, but also through personally ministering to others.

Don't imagine that you have to be a person who stirs up demons by your very presence as Jesus did. It may be that you are to demonstrate God's power in your life by building a frame for a building on your church property. Everything you do will be covered up eventually by someone else's work, but you do it to God's glory as you go. That's demonstration. If you lead hospitality and you not only talk about greeting people but you're right there actually greeting them, that's demonstration. If you not only lead prayer events, but personally pray with people and receive prayer ministry as God leads you, that's demonstration.

Explanation

There is no good thing that cannot be taken as an excuse to avoid another good thing. Take for example the call to witness by one's life. It's a good thing to witness by the way that we live, but there are many Christians who take that as an excuse for never witnessing with words. One good thing becomes an excuse to avoid another.

Some leaders and mentors get the idea that demonstration is a good thing. They're right. But they also get the idea that all you have to do is demonstrate and let someone else watch. That's not right. Demonstrating becomes the excuse to avoid doing the hard work of explaining the reasons for what you do.

Jesus taught by the use of parables. Parables challenge our thinking and carry us much further than simple statements of rules. But sometimes people misunderstand even the clearest of statements, and parables are not the clearest of statements. So Jesus takes the time to explain at least a part of his meaning to the disciples. Demonstration is good. Challenging thinking is good. Nonetheless, sometimes you need to explain yourself.

Check out how Jesus does this in Mark 4:1-12 as he tells a story and then explains its meaning (verse 13 and following).

Delegate

After much demonstration Jesus decides it's time to send his disciples out to practice what he has taught them.

> *7 Then he called together his twelve apostles and sent them*
> *out two by two with power over evil spirits. 8 He told them,*
> *"You may take along a walking stick. But don't carry food*
> *or a traveling bag or any money. 9 It's all right to wear*
> *sandals, but don't take along a change of clothes. 10 When*
> *you are welcomed into a home, stay there until you leave*

that town. [11] If any place won't welcome you or listen to your message, leave and shake the dust from your feet [i] as a warning to them." – Mark 6:7-11

Now here's something leaders often miss: Jesus sent them out. He didn't go with them. He didn't send spies to check on them. He gave them a task and expected them to do it.

I'm not suggesting that you should be stupid or use poor judgment in choosing the people you send out. But very often leaders wonder why people don't take authority and exercise initiative when the problem can be traced right back to the leader who is unwilling to let people go, make mistakes, and learn from them.

The apostles (ones who were sent out) were even surprised by what they accomplished on their mission. Even after seeing Jesus do all these things they weren't fully expecting what happened. The people you mentor will often be surprised at what they can do without you. Rejoice when someone learns that he or she doesn't really need you any more!

Empower

A critical part of delegation is empowerment—the authority, the permission, and the ability to act. The ability is given by God. You will often have to pass the authority and the permission on to the people you mentor.

Notice the results:

[12] The apostles left and started telling everyone to turn to God. [13] They forced out many demons and healed a lot of sick people by putting olive oil on them. – Mark 6:12-13

It happened! Now the disciples themselves have a new testimony—something to talk about!

Meditate

Finally, we have to look back on what we have done. Look how Jesus did it:

> [30] *After the apostles returned to Jesus, they told him everything they had done and taught.* [31] *But so many people were coming and going that Jesus and the apostles did not even have a chance to eat. Then Jesus said, "Let's go to a place where we can be alone and get some rest." – Mark 6:30-31*

My wife and I have discovered that this time of discussion and self-examination is important. It's not a time to beat yourself up about what went wrong, but rather a time to look forward at what can be done better. Many times ministry teams have told us that the time of discussion after the event was over was the most important element of a teaching event for them.

Consider what you have learned.

Conclusion

The purpose of Christian teaching is NOT:

- ✔ To make followers of the teacher
- ✔ Just to impart information
- ✔ To take away students' individuality
- ✔ To make students stop questioning

The purpose of Christian education IS:

- ✔ To bring students closer to God
- ✔ To bring students closer to one another
- ✔ To make them disciples of Jesus Christ.

Appendix A: Outline of the Participatory Study Method

How can I get more from my Bible reading?

There is no shortcut in Bible study. If you want to find what God has for you in scripture you will have to dig. There are some things you can do to make your study time more profitable. This brochure outlines an approach to Bible study which can help you both with devotional reading and with deeper study.

Preparation

Gather Materials — have pen, paper, highlighters or other markers and all materials you will need for study available.

Conditions — Find a place where you can study. If you study well with music playing, put some on. If you prefer quiet, arrange for a quiet place.

Resources — Get a small, well-selected set of study materials. See below under "Resources" for some suggestions.

Prayer

Pray specifically for an open mind to understand, an open heart to receive, enabling grace for the actions you will need to take.

Claim these promises:

> *But if we confess our sins to God, he can always be trusted to forgive us and take our sins away. – 1 John 1:9*
>
> *I will sprinkle you with clean water, and you will be clean and acceptable to me. I will wash away everything that makes you unclean, and I will remove your disgusting idols. I will take away your stubborn heart and give you a new heart and a desire to be faithful. You will have only pure thoughts, because I will put my Spirit in you and make you eager to obey my laws and teachings. – Ezekiel 36:25-27*

Get an Overview of the Passage

Read the passage multiple times. I use 12 or more, but any number from 3 times up will help.

Memorizing is useful, at least of key texts. (This will also require you to select key texts.) Read from different Bible versions, to help you with your concentration and to open up different ways of understanding the passage.

At this point **don't** use commentaries, study notes, your concordance, anything which takes your concentration off of the passage you are studying.

Study the Background

Find out who wrote the passage, to whom it was written, what is the situation being addressed, and what type of literature it is.

Meditate, Question, Research, Compare (Repeat as needed)

Meditate on the passage. If you are having difficulty meditating, think about telling someone else about the passage, such as a friend in need of encouragement, someone who is unsaved, or a child. Think: What questions might they ask about this passage? You can formulate thought questions or fact questions. Fact questions are about what the author is actually saying. Thought questions may lead you to other revelations well beyond the intended statement of the passage.

You can use outlining at this stage, comparison to other scriptures, to writers in church history, or to current experience. Ask: What similar experience are we having today? Can this help me understand the passage. For example, if you have had a vision will that help you understand Ezekiel's vision in Ezekiel 1? Ask your friends about experiences they have had.

Some historical writers you might consult include Jerome, Aquinas, Augustine, Martin Luther, John Wesley, John Calvin, Charles Spurgeon and many, many others.

Share your Thoughts

Ask yourself how this has applied in your experience. Get to know the person you are sharing with. Share your experience and then the text. Always work from your own **personal** experience with God.

Store up the experiences your friends share with you to use in studying further scripture.

Example Passage

1 Kings 19:11-18

1. Begin your study with prayer.
2. Read the passage several times. Can you tell this story in your own words?
3. Read 1 Kings 17-19. Check a Bible Handbook or study Bible for the background of 1 Kings.
4. Consider how Elijah feels through this experience. Consider what God is trying to accomplish by giving Elijah these experiences.
    - ✗ How did Elijah know the Lord was not in the wind, the earthquake or the fire?
    - ✗ Can the Lord appear in such violent events? (Use your concordance, looking up wind, fire, and earthquake.)
    - ✗ Does God respond to Elijah's complaint? (Only indirectly; he gives him a task.)
    - ✗ Is Elijah as much alone as he feels he is? (No, there are 7,000 more faithful people, v. 18.)
    - ✗ What other Bible characters have experienced something similar to this? (Daniel 3—the fiery furnace.)
    - ✗ What people in church history may have experienced something similar to this? (Any martyr or person who has suffered persecution.)
    - ✗ Have you experienced similar feelings?
    - ✗ Have you ever felt completely alone in your faith?
5. Share your experiences!!

Example Prayer for Bible Study

Lord, take from me any thought habits which will keep me from hearing. Make me open to your voice and your voice alone.

Lord, help me to accept your people as my brothers and sisters in your kingdom let me learn and grow from both their weaknesses and their strengths.

Lord, I trust you to reveal yourself to your people the way you know is best. Let your will be done.

Lord, let me not only recognize but obey your voice. Let my actions be conformed to your will. Help me to love my neighbor as myself.

In Jesus' name, Amen.

Resources

Reviews and/or notes on each of these resources are available on the Energion Publications web site, along with articles on how to use many of them. You can start from the following URL:

http://energion.com/books/biblical/study_tools.shtml.

Bible(s)

- For quick reading (overview):
  Contemporary English Version
  The Message
  New Living Translation (NLT)
- For study or reading:
  New International Version (NIV)
  Revised English Bible (REB)
- For study:
  New Revised Standard Version (NRSV)

(This list is not exhaustive.)

Bible Dictionaries

HarperCollins Bible Dictionary

New International Bible Dictionary

Concordances

The NIV Exhaustive Concordance.

Bibles with study notes

Oxford Study Bible (REB)

The Learning Bible (CEV)

Holy Spirit Encounter Bible (NLT)

Bible Atlases

Many study Bibles include good Bible atlases, but a separate Bible Atlas or world history atlas can be useful.

Oxford Bible Atlas

The Harper Atlas of World History

Bible Handbooks

The Cambridge Companion to the Bible

Zondervan Handbook to the Bible

For further information see the Energion Publications brochures *What's in a Version, Bible Study Tools* and *The Authority of the Bible*, found in the "pamphlets" directory of our web site.

Starting on the next page, you will find the *Participatory Study Method Worksheet* to help you in planning lessons on the major Biblical passages related to spiritual gifts. You can feel free to make copies of this sheet, or to download it in PDF 8 ½ x 11 format which will print on both sides of an ordinary sheet of paper. The URL is http://www.deepbiblestudy.com/worksheet.pdf.

The major passages on spiritual gifts are:

1 Corinthians 12-14

Ephesians 4:1-16

Romans 12

Participatory Study Method Worksheet

Supplies:

Besides the standard supplies used for your entire study, are there any special supplies you would like to use in studying this particular passage?

Prayer:

List any particular attitudes you would like to examine, or any particular requests for prayer.

Reading:

What Bible versions do you intend to use in reading? List them, and check them off as you complete your reading. Under each version make notes on any particular understanding you got from that time through the passage. Remember to include questions you may want to check on later, including particular translations you might wish to compare.

Bible Version	Read	Notes

Background:

Writer:____

Audience:______________________________________

Describe the situation:_____________________________________

Type of Literature: Poem Song/Hymn Story History Parable Allegory Doctrine Wisdom Prophecy Vision Prayer Letter Other

Note:____

____

Study:

Meditation – Note your questions and preliminary thoughts here. Don't be critical of your thoughts at this point. Just make notes and examine them later.

Outline – List three key points from your passage here. If you make a full outline, write it on another sheet of paper.

1.____

2.____

3.____

Comparison – List keywords first:

What other passages deal with the same subject? Be sure to use your concordance and the keywords you listed above.

Research – List resources and your notes from them.

Question or Application	Resource	Notes

Comparing with Current Experience:

Application	Source	Notes

Sharing:

List anyone you can share your thoughts from this passage with.

____

____

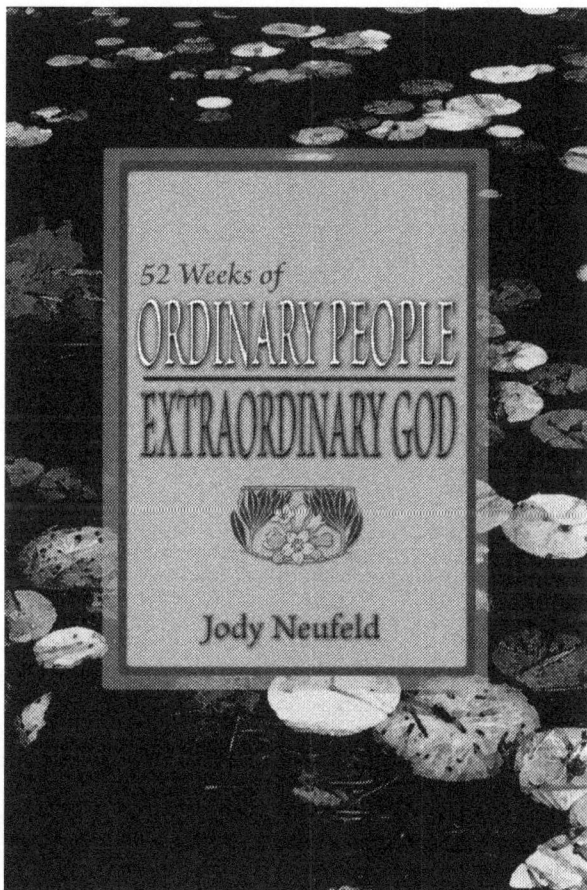

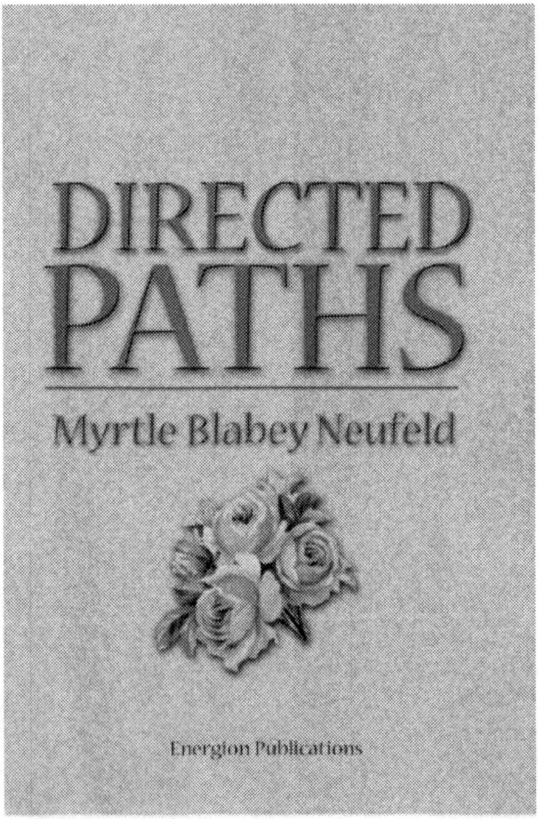
DIRECTED
PATHS
Myrtle Blabey Neufeld
Energion Publications

Participatory Study Series Pamphlets

Energion Publications publishes a number of pamphlets on the gifts of the Spirit and related topics. These can be used in outreach and in Christian education programs. They are especially useful as handouts.

Some titles are:

- ✓ I Want the Baptism of the Holy Spirit
  An outline on this important and controversial topic.
- ✓ Gifts and Offices
  Learning to understand gifts and how they prepare one for particular positions of responsibility in the church.
- ✓ Spiritual Gifts: Prophecy
- ✓ Spiritual Gifts: Speaking in Tongues
- ✓ Spiritual Gifts: Leadership
- ✓ Spiritual Gifts: Encouragement
- ✓ Spiritual Gifts: Helping
- ✓ Spiritual Gifts: Healing
- ✓ Spiritual Gifts: Miracles
- ✓ Seven Barriers to Hearing the Word
  Listening is the key to this approach to spiritual gifts. Do you know how to listen for the Holy Spirit?
- ✓ I Want to Pray!
  Basics of prayer as communion with God.

All pamphlets are available in PDF and Microsoft Word format and can be downloaded and printed in any quantity desired. You can also order them from us preprinted if you prefer not to print them yourself. Check out these resources at;

`http://www.participatorystudyseries.com`

Forthcoming from Energion Publications

Participating in the Bible – The basic guide to the participatory study method. Learn to understand the Bible for yourself, and to share your understanding with others. Watch our web site for availability.

When People Speak for God – Henry Neufeld examines inspiration and the gift of prophecy. How can you tell when someone's claim to speak for God is valid? What is the difference between scripture and the spoken word of God? Watch our web site for availability.

Becoming a Follower of Jesus – A short guide for the new believer. This resource is designed for churches as a tool to give to new believers and new members who want to thoroughly cover the basics of walking with Jesus. Available March, 2007.

Watch for the following participatory study guides:

- ✓ First Epistle to the Corinthians
- ✓ Acts
- ✓ Isaiah

Check our web site, www.energionpubs.com, for further information and release dates.

www.ingramcontent.com/pod-product-compliance
Lightning Source LLC
LaVergne TN
LVHW011204080426
835508LV00007B/595